NEW LIGHT

12 Quaker Voices

First published by O Books, 2008
O Books is an imprint of John Hunt Publishing Ltd., The Bothy, Deershot Lodge, Park Lane, Ropley,
Hants, SO24 0BE, UK
office1@o-books.net
www.o-books.net

Distribution in:	South Africa
	Alternative Books
UK and Europe	altbook@peterhyde.co.za
Orca Book Services	Tel: 021 555 4027 Fax: 021 447 1430
orders@orcabookservices.co.uk	
Tel: 01202 665432 Fax: 01202 666219	Text copyright Quaker Quest 2008
Int. code (44)	
	Design: Stuart Davies
USA and Canada	
NBN	ISBN: 978 1 84694 143 6
custserv@nbnbooks.com	
Tel: 1 800 462 6420 Fax: 1 800 338 4550	All rights reserved. Except for brief quotations
	in critical articles or reviews, no part of this
Australia and New Zealand	book may be reproduced in any manner without
Brumby Books	prior written permission from the publishers.
sales@brumbybooks.com.au	
Tel: 61 3 9761 5535 Fax: 61 3 9761 7095	The rights of the contributors as authors have
	been asserted in accordance with the
Far East (offices in Singapore, Thailand,	Copyright, Designs and Patents Act 1988.
Hong Kong, Taiwan)	
Pansing Distribution Pte Ltd	
kemal@pansing.com	A CIP catalogue record for this book is available
Tel: 65 6319 9939 Fax: 65 6462 5761	from the British Library.

Printed by Digital Book print

O Books operates a distinctive and ethical publishing philosophy in
all areas of its business, from its global network of authors to
production and worldwide distribution.
This book is produced on FSC certified stock, within ISO14001
standards. The printer plants sufficient trees each year through
the Woodland Trust to absorb the level of emitted carbon in
its production.

NEW LIGHT

12 Quaker Voices

edited by
Jennifer Kavanagh

BOOKS

Winchester, UK
Washington, USA

CONTENTS

ACKNOWLEDGEMENTS

The authors of this book, from whom the twelve voices for each section were drawn, are Terri Banks, William Barnes, Marjorie Boye-Anawomah, Mary Jo Clogg, Alec Davison, Geoffrey Durham, Val Ferguson, Andrew Herbert, Anne Hosking, Jean Jenn, Mike Jenn, Jennifer Kavanagh, Marie Lasenby, Simon Pollitt, Susan Seymour, Anna Sharman, Simon Watson, Audrey West and Martin Wilkinson.

We would like to acknowledge the support of Hampstead Monthly Meeting of the Religious Society of Friends, and of the Joseph Rowntree Charitable Trust.

To all, thanks.

PREFACE

This book has its origin in seven booklets written and produced since 2004 by a group of Quakers. The writers are active in Quaker Quest, a series of open meetings for people interested in a spiritual path for today which is simple, radical and contemporary: the Quaker way. The project began in London in 2002 and now Quaker Quest events are held throughout Britain and, increasingly, in North America, Australasia and Europe.

Each part of this book comprises twelve short personal reflections on themes which are of importance to enquirers and which stand at the heart of the Quaker faith. The writers in each section agreed that no one should see anyone else's contribution until all twelve were completed, and all pieces remain anonymous.

We hope that *New Light: 12 Quaker voices* will be a help to those seeking meaning and purpose in their lives.

INTRODUCTION

"Are you open to new light from whatever source it may come?"

Advices & Queries

The starting point of this book is a spiritual path

- that welcomes the continuing revelation of new truth
- that is not confined by dogma and creed but liberated in personal experience
- that depends upon the mutual responsibility of all its members
- that is a way of life centred in the understanding that there is no time but the present
- that treats the world and its peoples as sacred
- that refuses to condone the killing of others in war or for punishment
- that believes in equality before God
- that sustains a lively community engaged in helping to heal a broken world.

Quakers (or the Religious Society of Friends, to give us our proper name) emerged in Britain some 350 years ago from the tumult of the Civil War and a period of religious turmoil. The Society was radical then, in its return to what it understood to be the way of early Christians, its emphasis on God within, and its valuing of the individual's relationship to God over the dogma, rituals and symbols of the traditional churches. It remains radical today. Rooted in Christianity, we try to be "open to new light"; we do not claim to have found the only truth; indeed, we benefit from the power and wisdom not only of the different denominations of Christianity, but of other faiths.

The centre of the Quaker way is the Meeting for Worship, a meeting of equals in stillness and silence, waiting on God, listening to the Spirit. There is no priestly leader, with a special role or status: we all share the responsibility for our worship and our faith. We base what we believe on our own experience, not on what we have been told. We try to be true to ourselves, to the God within each of us.

The simplicity, equality, peace and truth of the Meeting for Worship underpin the way we try to live our lives. Sitting in stillness, we wait to hear what Love requires of us in the mending of our world.

This is a contemporary spiritual path. We believe that it has relevance for independent-minded seekers after the Truth, and that its values of nonviolence and open-mindedness are a necessary and inspiring contribution to a fragmented and divided world.

The short pieces in this book can provide material for daily private contemplation, or form the basis for study by discussion groups. The twelve voices heard here represent a diversity of experience and belief revealing a fundamental unity. We hope that they will shed new light on a spiritual path that is simple, radical and contemporary – a path that is open to all.

WHAT IS GOD?

We may seem at times to take God for granted. But we know the beyond in our midst; we rely on grace, on God's free, sustaining, creative and lively action as we rely on the air we breathe and the ground we walk on.

Quaker Faith & Practice, 26.66

1

Years ago, at the end of an evening's informal group discussion, I heard myself saying, "Well, with my back against the wall, all I can say is: 'For me God Is'."

Now, nearly forty years later, I find myself saying exactly the same thing. Whether I understand any better what I mean by that statement I sometimes wonder. What I do know is that no matter what questions arise, I find myself responding from the same position. It is a position that has become a part of my reality, a part of my being. At the same time it is not a position I could expect anyone else to hold, for I see each of us as being our own authority, finding our own way. I would say that in some ways I feel I am still at the beginning, that the freshness of discovery can be there every moment of every day.

I was brought up in a home where traditional Christian teaching prevailed. Of course I asked questions, and as life went on I found fewer and fewer satisfactory answers. Like so many others I found myself unable to accept much of what seemed important in the practice of my church. In retrospect I think that for me the external practice hid the truth. Eventually, after some really hard searching, I was confronted with the truth. With the word God.

As a child my understanding of this word was built up from being told that God was everywhere but couldn't be seen. I have to say that I was not given any sense of God being a frightening or punishing figure. Today my sense of God has, I am sure, grown from that early teaching, which both satisfied and puzzled me as a child. Of course there was a time when I thought of God as a kind of person, but that understanding is not mine now, although I respect those who walk hand in hand with a personal God.

My understanding of this reality in my life is very simple. I think of absolute love, of total goodness. Of a power which is beyond and is too great for my complete apprehension, yet is part of me, and of all others. A power that humbles and yet enhances. A power that allows absolute freedom yet is there always, even if sometimes hard to find. The words "seeker after the Truth" are so important to me.

I believe that each of us must find his or her own way, that we must be open to the light, which may mean that we discard long-cherished understandings or make surprising and entrancing discoveries. In my experience, it has been in the most surprising places and from seemingly the most unlikely sources that I find God being revealed. This can be when I truly encounter that of God in another, or in the world, or just suddenly entering my mind. Truth for me is the personal encounter with the Divine, with God. Those times when, in the stillness, all is well. When I am carried on the breath of the spirit.

2

I need God in the same way that I need food, drink and sleep. I am absolutely sure that needing God is an integral part of the human condition, and that some people find it harder than others to accept it. They, in their turn, of course, know that I am deluding myself. I believe in God. David Steindl-Rast has said that God is a name for a reality which cannot be named, and that is the closest definition I have ever encountered for the indefinable. For me, God is a reality. I believe in God because I experience it.

It wasn't always that way for me. I spent about thirty years of my life unsure and angry and in a fog. I think now that I was struggling not to believe. I remember sitting next to a man in a self-help group that I was attending, and finding myself seething with unexpressed anger when he said, "Ego stands for Easing God Out." "How dare you question my ego?" I thought. "I need my ego. My ego has brought me the success I've had."

Yet that encounter must have stirred some truth inside me. Three weeks later I sought the man out and asked him in detail what he meant. I wanted to know how he had come to his view, what practice he was adopting, how he could possibly cope with his life without resorting to the power of self.

He made some simple, perhaps naïve, suggestions. He suggested that humility was a better coping mechanism in life than ego. He told me that I would find it easier to understand my life if I were able to key into an energy that was greater than me. He told me that his life had been changed by some simple practices, and that I could begin to adopt them if I wanted to.

I'm constantly astonished by our capacity to turn unbelief into belief. It is as if we are simply flipping a coin. Certainly, that was how it was for me.

I decided not to worry about defining the power I was trying to align myself with. I resolved to get on my knees as I had when I was a child, and burble quietly. I burbled to the child I had been when I was born, that perfect baby boy. I burbled to the force that gave me life. If I wasn't sure about how to pray to God, I could at least burble to Good, so I did that. Quite quickly, over the next three or four weeks, my life began to change utterly. I was undergoing a religious conversion. And it was a surprisingly simple matter.

I won't dwell on the many ways in which my life was up-ended, because they really aren't the point. What matters is that I turned to something outside myself and I changed – *but I had to ask to do it.*

It is a strange phenomenon that as we ask to move closer to God, God moves closer to us, and when we move away, God becomes harder and harder to discern. Could it be that this great energy is the quintessence of selflessness, as well as of love and truth and the force for good? Well, yes, I think so. That has certainly been my experience. God became a reality for me only because I asked it to.

As a result of these experiences, I fail utterly to understand the argument that "If there were a God there wouldn't be any wars", or "What's God doing about the famine in Ethiopia?" Surely, it is we who cause these difficulties when we fail to align ourselves to the power of God. It is for us to solve them. And we will, if we collectively acquire the humility to ask.

I have stopped praying to Good now. The God that I pray to is inside me, and outside me. When I ask to touch it, it becomes tangible. When I ask for help, I get it, and never in ways that I expect. When I forget about it, it disappears from view.

At best it is a warmth, a real presence in my life. But it can be a disturbing one, too. Belief in God demands change – constant, demanding and sometimes fundamental change. Often I feel painted into corners, as if I am being forced by God to do things against my will. When I fight these impulses (that ego again!) the result is a feeling of cruel disorientation and a lonely understanding that my will was wrong. When I allow the spirit to guide me against my judgement, I change. There emerges a calm in my life. I stop fighting. I feel completely human again.

3

My experience of God is of a force. It is within me, and outside me, omnipresent in the world. It has been with me since childhood, although it has taken years for me to recognise it and to try to express it, and, especially, to be sensitive and responsive to it. I can go for some time without acknowledging it, but it will not leave me alone. It is a force of light and piercing truth; it is a force of love, compassion and mercy. When the force moves through me, compelling me to act, it will not be denied.

This force can be experienced; it can be felt, and that which I feel, I describe as the voice of God, but it is really more a prodding of God. If I sit in stillness, truly opening myself to the prodding, it can rise up within me. I cannot call it up at will, even with great effort; it comes in its own time and when it will, and when it does I describe it as the grace of God. If I sit in stillness with others, in a worshipping group, it can come to us all as a group. When I am entirely open to this force I describe it, in the words of the first commandment, as "loving the Lord my God with all my heart and all my mind and all my soul". The second commandment, "to love my neighbour as myself", follows automatically.

The force that is God is an absolute ethic: that of the second commandment. It calls upon me to exercise love and mercy and to act justly to my fellow beings. Any form of cruelty or killing, anything which diminishes another, is inimical to God. God is total understanding, and all that is understood must be forgiven. In so far as we live in the light of God, we are forgiving. We can but do our best to live within this ethic.

I cannot envisage this force as anthropomorphic. It has not come to humankind magically into a single body at a single point in history. It is always present, waiting to be recognised, in every precious, unique human being, every child of God. Each of us has the potential to act as a conduit of this force. God does not target me, as an individual, or instruct me personally. The God force is always there in all of us at all times. I experience this as a personal message when the force, the light, breaks through in my heart. This grace of God might be experienced by anyone at any time.

I can feel the force of God's light at unexpected moments: as I walk down the street, as a stranger smiles in a crowd, as I look at the sky. I feel the power of God in the vastness of the universe, in the minuteness of a grain of sand. I experience my life both as brief as the day-lily's and yet as a part of the aeons of history. God is manifest in this relativity of time.

As I give thanks for the measure of God that has been granted to my awareness, I pray that it may continue and that I may not fail to respond as a faithful servant.

4

The Akans of Ghana have a saying: *Obi nkyere akodaa Nyame*. "You don't have to tell a child that there is God because it already knows." I suppose that's how I feel – that God is.

I feel God as a power to be drawn on and from which to receive strength. Sometimes in my life, when all else has failed, I have prayed for this strength and felt at peace.

When I was a child I heard a story about a missionary in the South Seas who was composing a sermon and was finding it difficult to translate "trust in God", until a tired visitor arrived, and, sinking down into a chair, said, in the local language: "How good it is to rest my full weight on this seat." There was the translation, and I feel that's how it is.

I can believe in God as an originator of life, the universe, etc., which has been left to evolve, but as for the inventor or the creator of individual species, then – why the cockroach?

5

"Do you believe in God?" is a question I imagine being asked by people like Richard Dawkins, who loves to debate the issue in his wonderful books about evolution. His chosen antagonists seem to be fundamentalists for whom God is a supernatural creator, father, and judge. The question puts me on the defensive. I want to answer: "Well, it depends what you think God is."

That doesn't seem a very good place to start.

Then there's the word "believe", which seems to denote something asserted in the face of contradictory evidence. Yet we say that Quakerism is experiential. If I have experienced something, I know it; I don't have to "believe" it.

So I am going to start somewhere else, with faith. Quakers call their book of guidance and inspiration *Quaker Faith & Practice*. Faith is a word I feel comfortable with. I know I have faith. Faith is what gets me out of bed in the morning and it determines what I do, my practice.

Faith in what?

I say that there is such a thing as "worth". That everything is not relative, or expedient. That some things and actions are better than others. I see an endless struggle between forces for good on the one hand and evil and apathy on the other. My faith is not a blind belief that good will overcome evil and despair in the end and that all will be perfect, but rather that good energy will always be there, bringing its blessings, and that I can obtain joy by doing my bit to share those blessings and that love with others.

Faith is about there being meaning in my life, from knowing that I am not just an isolated individual, but part of a whole, and that I have my place and role within that.

The theologian Mary Daly has written, "Why indeed must 'god' be a noun? Why not a verb ... the most active and dynamic of all?" I agree with that. I can live with the term God as energy, force, direction, rather than a thing or a person.

Another metaphor for God is a ball of many mirrored facets. We all see a part of it, and what we see reflects back to us a unique perspective, which is a true reflection yet only part of the whole. In this way, I can accept that others will have a different view of God, different words for God, different experiences of God, and yet all these are but glimpses of fragments of the same thing, which is greater than anything we can comprehend.

These are some of the fragments I see:

Photographs of our precious, tiny, green planet, in the vastness and darkness of space. Surely, we have to stick together and care for one another and our common home, or we are nothing. Some people I know can contemplate the heavens and stars and infinity of space and find solace, strength and inspiration from that. I can't quite get that far yet. My faith is rather earth-bound, even tied to humanity, rather than other forms of life.

Mountains that have the power to take me out of myself, out of the now. I know that mountains are not eternal, but they seem immovable, unperturbed by storms, human settlement and extraction of logs or minerals. In the words of the psalm: "I raise my eyes unto the hills from whence my help comes." God is more eternal than mountains.

Great music. Many composers, writers, painters speak of what they create as coming from God through them. I find sacred choral music takes me the closest I get to a sense of awe, wonder, praise and of the tenderness of the Divine.

A leaf on a tree. The leaf buds and opens, doing its bit for the growth of the tree, creating oxygen. Then, the leaf withers and dies and falls to the ground, still contributing to the nourishment of the soil, and the tree lives on.

So I have faith that it is worth my doing something. But how to decide what to do? Here I have found Quakers offer a method. To be still enough to listen, and to share and support one another. But who or what am I listening to? Do I hear anything? How do I know that a thought I have is a leading from God?

People ask, "If God is an all-powerful force, then why can't it stop pain and suffering, fear and war?" If God is the energy, then it is trying to stop these things. And if God is in us, then we must be part of the effort to stop them.

I am on a journey, a path that winds around a mountain; I see the same thing from different perspectives all the time. But I know there is a path, that it leads somewhere, and that there is a force that is moving me along it.

6

To define or to describe God is to distort, to impose our own limitations of time and space. I can only give my own experience thus far.

I experience God as the life-force, the spark of the Divine, not dualistically a creator, but immanent: the One manifest in the many. All the richness and variety of the natural world is an expression of God. "Every creature is a word of God", as the medieval mystic, Meister Eckhart, said. I experience God both in the uniqueness of living creatures – the birdness of a bird, the treeness of a tree – and in that which brings us together: the unifying and connecting principle between and within all creation, the movement in our hearts at the beauty of the natural world, the joy of recognition in the eyes of another human being. God as relationship.

I experience God as Being, unlimited by time or space. Our dream world, sense of *déjà vu*, or ecstatic experiences when all seems gathered in a present moment, are intimations of divine eternity, as are the stars, which we see millions of years after they are shown to us.

I experience God as purpose, a purpose in which we participate, in a continuing process of creation, transformation, resurrection and revelation.

I experience God as a presence in my heart and in my bowels, in the depths of my being; in the desert and in the tiniest chapel; in music and dance as well as in the stillness and silence; in joy and anguish, darkness and light. In the indivisibility of God we understand the connectedness of opposites.

God is a guiding force in my life. Until recently I could not feel God as love, but I have come to an understanding recently that the love is in the relationship, the connectedness which I experience consciously through others and, vividly, unexpectedly, through acts of synchronicity. Glimpses of connections that I had not previously understood: connections that show me the way, affirm my steps on the path, nurture me, not with the cuddly limited love of my imaginings, but with the mature love and acceptance of my real self.

Prayer for me is largely a matter of adoration and thankfulness. In terms of the events of my life and that of others, it is rarely petitionary or intercessionary, except in moments of extremity. When facing the foreknowledge of the Divine, only "Thy Will be Done" seems appropriate. I strive for the state of grace that was expressed by a member of my Quaker Meeting, who said, "I want to thank God for everything, including the things I didn't want."

7

From very young I have been awe-struck by experiences I had no name for. As I grew up I came to understand these in terms of God. Quakers use many words for God – Spirit, the Divine, etc. – perhaps because they have associated the word with some, now unacceptable, picture of a vengeful old man in the sky. I have always used God because that is the word with which I am most comfortable. It represents for me in its many translations the way humans have sought to give a name to explain the spiritual and the moral. So I shall use God, and I hope it will not be a barrier for you.

What I have learned is that I experience this God as both closer than breath (and quite alarmingly personal and loving!) and yet also as infinite, creative and unknowable.

I meet this God, often unexpectedly – in joy, in suffering, occasionally in nature, in the most minute particulars of daily life, and often in people. Indeed, it is often in the least likely people that I catch a glimpse of their goodness, their "Godness".

I encounter, rather than believe in, God. But I have chosen, and it is a choice, to bet my life (literally) on the power, the love, the challenge, that I call God. For me it has always been a stark choice. You take it seriously (or try to) twenty-four hours a day or not at all. Like pregnancy, there are no half measures – I can no more be "a little bit religious" than "a little bit pregnant"!

It is not easy. I go for long periods with grave doubt. There was at least one time in my life when I was not just agnostic but quite sure that there was no God. "Life's a bitch and then you die" seemed to me to be the most realistic assessment of everything. But somehow, so far, I haven't cancelled the bet.

There are those who will feel that the sum of the divine sparks in everyone is all that any God can be; for others, the divine they encounter is a power but seems unlikely to have anything to do with the creation and sustaining of the universe. I'm probably amongst those who suspect that the God I encounter is even more than the creator and sustainer.

I am always mindful of the old story of the blind men describing the elephant. One holds the tail and suggests the animal is like a rope, another feels the side and says it is more like a wall. One holding the leg says it must be a tree, while another at the trunk insists on it resembling a snake. Can we ever really know all of the nature of God?

This is expressed well in a complex Hindu concept – *sarvadhar-masambhava*. This says that as a result of one's own experience of the ultimate we may be able to understand a similar experience of another and respect it. But from this deep experience of ultimateness and universality at the depth of one's own religious faith what results is not a superficial suggestion that "all religions are the same", but a capacity to understand that the experience of another may be equally ultimate and universal but quite different from one's own. We may recognise the validity of the encounter yet not recognize the God of whom the other speaks. This is a religious tolerance based on a deep respect, "the homage which the finite mind pays to the inexhaustibility of the infinite," in the words of Radhakrishnan.

I think this is very important to remember. And yet, and yet... There is a paradox. When I speak with my friend who is a devout Muslim, we find that as we talk of our lives and our work, as we move beyond the words to the spaces in between them and truly let those moments of attentiveness to each other address us, so we find a deep unity in our encounter with God ("closer than our jugular vein", as the Koran says).

And it is in that hospitality of listening and waiting that we Quakers can find our unity with one another amidst the very different words we use.

8

"The song of the Spirit is everywhere": its melody resonates throughout my experience and its lyric haunts my attempts at understanding.

This *experience* of the Divine comes to me unexpectedly in flashes, sudden openings, when the penny drops, or things click into place. This is a glimpse of the other, "rumours of angels", a tangential glancing blow of the holy. No Damascus visions or burning bushes, but humble occasions which I recognise, often long afterwards, as times of inner enlargement when my own spirit has magnified or manifested something greater.

The ground-swell burden of these Spirit experiences rises from the heart of the caring and loving I have known from being a much-wanted child and a well-accepted partner in a merry marriage. From profound family illnesses and the deaths of parents, sister and friends to the anxieties and joys of the births of children and grandchildren there have been myriad times when I have touched the transcendent in laughter and loneliness, in the sensualities of the flesh and the companionship of loved ones, in breakdown and breakthrough. And so I learned to trust life and to feel that I belonged.

The tunes in counterpoint sing of a presence evoked through beauty and fear, in meadow and mountain, as child and teenager, birdwatching or camping under radiant stars, awe and wonder palpable. They echo from transformations in the absorption of play at any age when time stands still and my ego is lost in another medium – music, film, books or theatre-making. They resonate out of the stillness of worship following a deep experience by a now opened and bonded group.

But most revealing of the nature of the Spirit are those times of despair and hurt and meaninglessness, when life, I believed, was being unfair to me, or when the world, I felt, was grossly unjust and tragic to others, and I have needed to surrender myself to the creative powers within to heal and to reconcile or to lead me into new insights and new ways. This Power does not step in "over there", to intervene in calamity or holocaust, but it does melt a new pathway "in here", within myself.

I have found that my *understandings* of the song of the Spirit change my experiences, and these then call for new understandings. Just as the gods no longer speak through the thunderclouds now that we know of thermal air currents, so the concept of God no longer speaks to me at all. I cannot separate the word God from an anthropomorphic being, whether judge or father, lord or king, with a will that may be determined and known rather than a way of free choice.

So I lay down God as noun and take up the Spirit as verb – an eternal process, that is evolving and creative, genuinely open, free and without destination. For the Spirit itself evolves as the universe and humanity evolve; our spiritual quest is a story of new revelations. Experiencing this power of Spirit has been real for me, not a linguistic metaphor, so I look for a realistic understanding.

I read of the beginnings of the universe emanating from a point of singularity, like an exhalation from another state beyond our universe's dimensions, a quantum plenum full of infinite potential. In less than a split second an explosion of quantum riches expanded into a quantum energy field out of which all that is material has come and where, after its transitory manifestation as galaxy, star, dolphin or philosopher, will ultimately return. We are temporary negotiations of this final Truth: all is of the Spirit and in the Spirit; transcendence is shot through the immanent. This energy field is my divinity, the oneness and wholeness of all; matter *is* energy. I recognise it as sacred, so each of its expressions in our universe is sacred.

As energy resonating with the consciousness of our minds, which have evolved as its receptors, the Spirit is ultimately unknowable because it is chaotic and uncertain. But as matter, out of which humanity has been fashioned, it is eminently knowable through all our varieties of discourse. The prophet, artist, scientist and mystic equally reveal its principles, just as cancer, AIDS, penicillin and aspirin reveal the variety of its contingency. The Spirit knows no chosen people; everyone is a unique, experimental expression of the Divine, regardless of gender or colour or sexual orientation.

The Spirit is more than love, but it cannot be caged in dogma and creed. Yet I need a belief to live by which gives meaning and focus. When I am aligned to the way of the Spirit's freedom and in harmony with its principles then growth is healthy and true, not to be made perfect but to be fulfilled in my uniqueness. The soul, the heart, the light, the Christ, the seed are each universal notions of the source of this growth. I cannot escape from the embrace of the Spirit within me and all about me. My pride and self-centredness can block it out, but it is there waiting; its song resonates through me until I finally become one with it again.

9

In my life experience the Divine has been a reality. The God of love, compassion and tender upholding is one that I have known. But my God is not just personal; S/he is also power or energy, the Divine Source. This Divine Power is part of all creative energy, which cannot be defined or confined, just glimpsed in creation and creative forms. It is a mystical Other, in which and with which I am engaged. Jesus was someone who more clearly knew this Divine Spirit than most, and lived his life in joyful response to it.

The spiritual path towards awareness of the Divine is not one which is found through guilt, duty or conformity; rather it is known in the joy-filled wholeness of the full reality of life. This Divine Spirit, however, can invade my orderliness and jolt me; it pushes out the comfortable boundaries; it demands that I struggle to be in balance with it; it requires my response.

As we are all part of this known and unknown Divine Energy, so we are in relation to all others and to all created things; my self and my actions directly affect all else, so I am therefore an integrated part of the universal whole.

I believe that the power of prayer with God can bring about change, usually in subtle and longer-term ways, but sometimes in the immediate. I can also be transformed and changed by others' encounters with God, and also in what they write.

So, at the moment, my God finds expression in:

The joy of *The God of Surprises*;
The affirmation of *The Cloud of Unknowing*;
The comfort of Julian of Norwich in *A Revelation of Love*;
The awe of Thomas Kelly's *A Testament of Devotion*;
and the wonder of *The Coming of the Cosmic Christ*.
But this is an exploration, a journey; and how on this spiritual path may I yet come to know the Divine?

10

I have never really been sure about God. Throughout my childhood I really can't remember believing in God, but didn't positively disbelieve either. At school we sang hymns, and the only ones I remember being at all moved by were the ones about nature, particularly one that talks about the stars appearing in the evening, showing

myriad worlds unknown;
and man, the marvel seeing
forgets his selfish being
for joy of beauty not his own.

The sexist language didn't bother me back then, and even now this verse speaks to me. My Quaker parents encouraged me to look at the words of the hymns critically and decide for myself what I could accept.

I remember, perhaps as a student, formulating my belief like this: some impulse in me sometimes leads me to be generous, or unselfish, and other people talk about being led by God to this kind of goodness, so I might as well call the impulse I feel God as well.

I have always liked to spend time outdoors, especially on my own, and used to sit at the top of an apple tree, from where I could see the hills in the distance. I sometimes got an inspired kind of feeling in places like this, and still do, and this feeling seems to fit with other experiences that people call spiritual or religious or of God. It is a similar feeling to being deeply moved, for example by hearing someone's personal story or by a work of art or music, and I choose to call this feeling spiritual as well.

Sometimes I think I am verging on being atheist, because I think it is quite possible that the inspiring and leading God I believe in could be a product of my mind (and the minds of other people). The human brain is such a marvellous thing, full of mystery, that I don't think it is a problem to find one more mystery in it. But God may equally be outside us all – I really don't know. I don't spend much time worrying about theology – it is the inspiration and the impetus to change the world for the better that really matter.

One aspect that some people apply to God is one I have a problem with: the creator. I studied biology in order to find out more about how the wonderful world works, and the more I learnt about the evolution of life, the more wonderful I found it. But this wasn't wonder at what the divine creator had made, but an amazement that all this beauty and complexity can come about by entirely understandable processes, without outside intervention.

As a scientist I prefer rational explanations for things, if such explanations exist. Also, I don't think that believing in a creator God would help me in my life, whereas the inspiration and direction I get from the other aspects of the Divine are very helpful indeed. The idea of Mother Earth doesn't appeal to me either – it seems too simplistic to reduce the whole earth to one human-like character.

Strangely enough, I don't find the concept of God as either father or mother helpful very often, though occasionally I find myself needing to pray to a kind of parent figure. Once recently I found myself saying "Lord" when I wanted to talk to the Divine, which seemed odd given the patriarchal overtones of the word. But these days one hardly hears the word Lord in any context except for that of God, whereas the word God itself is over-used ("Oh, my God" is a phrase I use far too much, in a non-spiritual way).

One place where I feel God most strongly is in Quaker Meetings for Worship. In business meetings especially, which are based on silent waiting for God's leadings, I have felt the group being drawn to the best decision even when I or others strongly disagreed.

11

I am distressed when I read of yet another war about God's name, somewhere in God's world. What pain, what unimaginable grief the Creator must feel at this perversion of the creation.

I use many names for the Divine, sometimes lingering with one sacred name, but wary of becoming territorial, my god shrinking to mere possession. Early Quakers used Light, giving life and clarity, showing me the next steps, and Light is probably the word I use most of all.

In the Bible I do like God as mother hen sheltering her young, God as artisan, delighting in Wisdom (who is also God, and female), playing by God's side from the beginning of creation. John's gospel sees Wisdom as Jesus. Each word suggests different manifestations. When I was pregnant, the babyhood of God gave me hope and promise.

My experience is that God is beyond all our imagining, bigger than any one name we humans use. Dios, Gott, El, Yahweh, Allah, Ahura Mazda – I could never learn enough languages to pronounce all the names of God; I cannot in this life explore all these understandings.

I want to express my awe before the greatness of God, but have not – yet – found the vocabulary. I was not brought up in a country with a monarch, and cannot find any reality in Lord. Some cannot bear God as father or mother, for only cruelty and betrayal come to mind; perhaps those who have suffered need Friend, Comforter, Healer, Ground of Being, or Truth to me feel cold and abstract, yet feel warm to others – how wonderfully odd!

The early Quaker, George Fox, could have been speaking for me, when he said:

> Now where is this spirit, and where is this truth? Is it not within people?... And so every man and woman in the whole world must come to the spirit and truth in their own hearts, by which they must know the God of truth.

The words of Samuel Fisher, another early Quaker, excite me (though I would not use "he" or "she"):

> Ye query, what God really is in himself?... God, as he is really in himself, is beyond all definition of ours at all.

Beyond definition, yes, but there are limitations to my inclusive approach. I cannot accept the Maya and Aztec god, who demanded human sacrifice, the living hearts torn from captives and from their own children, offered daily to ensure the world did not end. I have difficulty even learning from this view of God. My approach to God is universal, but I realise some gods are not-God. I have to discriminate. The God I find to be real and whom I worship is just, loving, ethical, and much, much more, but not capricious or cruel.

This has turned into a love song to the One Who is my Life and my End (God is clearly Capital Letters too!).

12

What I worship, what is divine for me, is the fundamental Energy of on-going creation with its millions of worlds and trillions of beings. Through infinite time it is leading us towards a Consciousness when all things will share the same Mind.

Humanity is a speck of dust in all this, but as one amid the many I try to sense the direction of Consciousness and to live in response to it. That is our purpose. In any context we can each respond in ways that are more or less in line with it, with the spirit of it, the closer alignment elevating the "spirit in which we live".

One response is to be in awe of the sheer diversity from molecule to universe and of every expression of the Life-Force. Another is to celebrate progress towards fulfilling life's potential, including the developments of consciousness of self, of love and the ability to sacrifice self for that which is divine.

But these were not my first responses. Those were to respond to the love of those around me, and then to the teaching of Jesus about love and his expression of it. I saw its potential and experienced its life-enhancing power as I opened myself up to allow love to pass through me. Touched, humbled but elevated, not understanding or needing any explanation, from then I've worked out the implications in service, alive (in varying degrees) to the Energy around and within.

The ever-present Energy is there to be drawn on by anyone who opens himself or herself to it. It calls us in the direction of love and compassion, understanding and forgiveness, and whatever else supports the unity of life, from social inclusion on local and global scales to care of the natural environment. Opening yourself up is challenging, a direction which is in tension with the opposite drive to control your life, protect and enhance your position and become less vulnerable.

When I trust the relationship with the Energy, I can take risks and grow in faith. I try to develop my Consciousness through silent attention to it in a Quaker Meeting, open to inspiration and in company with others, as well as through reading and reflection.

This I find helpful in enabling me to respond to the Divine, especially as reflected in others, though my weakness is greater than my strength.

> *What are your thoughts about God?*
> *Why not try writing your own piece?*

WHY PACIFISM?

All bloody principles and practices we do utterly deny, with all outward wars, and strife, and fightings with outward weapons, for any end, or any pretence whatsoever, and this is our testimony to the whole world.

Quaker declaration to Charles II, 1660

1

My abhorrence of war is very deep seated, a truly gut feeling which I have had for as long as I can remember. There are many arguments and justifications that I can put forward to support this stance, as can all pacifists. I can say that peacemaking and nonviolence are intrinsically linked to my basic Quaker belief that every person has the capacity to know and love God, and that we are all unique, precious, children of God. I can quote biblical injunctions: thou shalt not kill; you are to love your neighbour as yourself. I can argue from history that violence only begets violence, and that no lasting peace has ever been built on violence and injustice.

But I believe that at the very root of my pacifism, and I believe of most others, is a compellingly strong feeling, not a reasoned argument but a feeling, that it is simply wrong to hurt another human being. The issue of war and violent resolution of conflict is to me a matter of black and white in an otherwise often grey world. War is wrong. Violence is wrong. Harming others is wrong. War is so heinous a crime that any nonviolent action to prevent or stop it is justified.

I am sickened when I see the country in which I live and work and pay taxes deploying its army to kill and destroy in distant lands. It is being done in my name; my tax money pays for it; I profit from the loot that is seized; I am responsible. I can no more evade my involvement than can those victims who are bombed, or shot dead while their homes are razed to the ground. They are harmed. I am responsible, and am myself harmed. We are all caught up in the jaws of war. Do not ask for whom the bells of war toll; they toll for every one of us.

As a pacifist I am often challenged on the issue of self-defence.

How would I respond if I, or my family or neighbours, were to be personally attacked? I don't think this question can be answered hypothetically, as none of us can be sure what instantaneous response we might make under sudden personal attack. My reaction might well be impulsive rather than cerebral. It's possible it would be violent, but it wouldn't be premeditated violence. I remember the fierce protective instinct that possessed me when I had a baby to care for, and how I was overwhelmed by the force of my emotions and reactions at that time.

This issue, however, is surely a long way from the war preparations of nations: the calculated stockpiling of weaponry of destruction; the training of young men and women in the arts of killing; the strategic military plans awaiting implementation. It's a long way from war and the readiness for war. And I like the response of the conscientious objector in the Second World War who was challenged as to how he would respond if his sister were to be raped by "the enemy". "Well," he said, "I wouldn't want to respond by bombing the rapist's sister."

Similar to the frequently asked question of self-defence is that of disarmament. "Would you really have our nation unilaterally lay down all arms and disband all military forces?" I am asked. Of course not. Effective disarmament would have to be a gradual process, achieved in concert among the nations of the world. It would require the leadership of men and women of vision in the militarised nations. They would have to recognise their nations' self-interest in reducing economic exploitation of weaker nations and in relinquishing military strength in order to strengthen world security. It would mean re-deploying national forces into international peacekeeping forces. Its success would depend on an arms-control system based upon fairness, not upon nuclear powers strengthening their own capacities while preaching non-proliferation to others. In short, it would depend upon trust, foresight, justice and respect – in fact, upon loving one's neighbour.

I like to think that some day humanity will view the wars of the twentieth and twenty-first centuries with the abhorrence with which we now view the gladiatorial contests of ancient Rome. People will wonder how human society could ever have tolerated the pitting in deadly combat of one group of young men, and now women, from one country against a similar group from another country. It will seem to them grotesque that massive resources were poured into lethal weaponry of death, destruction and torture while large segments of humanity went hungry and while simple illnesses went untreated. It will seem to them imperative to find nonviolent solutions to the perennial conflicts in the world, and to practise pacifism.

2

Quaker belief in peace derives from a specific event in 1660 – the declaration to Charles II when Quakers were accused of seeking to overthrow the government: "our principle is, and our practices have always been, to seek peace, and ensue it". But the coming of World War in 1914 and of conscription in 1916 made the need for a living testimony to peace – and to conscientious objection – more urgent. The horrors of the First World War, and the increasing likelihood of another one during the twenties and thirties, led Dick Sheppard, vicar of St. Martin-in-the-Fields and popular as "the radio parson", to launch in 1934 the Peace Pledge Union. Its declaration was "We renounce war and never again, directly or indirectly, will we support or sanction another." Membership grew steadily. Even in September 1939, when war was again declared, 2,435 new members joined; in October another 2,280. By April 1940 membership had risen to 136,000. It was not until the fall of France in May 1940 that numbers started to drop sharply.

The treatment of conscientious objectors in the First World War – many of whom suffered in prison – led the government in its 1939 Military Training Act (which re-introduced conscription) to provide for tribunals to decide about those claiming exemption as conscientious objectors. Between 1939 and 1945, more than 67,000 did so – nearly four times as many as in the earlier war. Six per cent of these were "absolutists" who refused to perform any compulsory alternative service. Friends, led by Arnold Rowntree and Paul Cadbury, decided to form again the Friends' Ambulance Unit, which had existed in the earlier war. Three hundred applied to join in the first few days, and priority was given to Friends and those who had attended Quaker schools. Throughout the war 5,000 people enquired about membership and 1,314, including 97 women, actually joined, "spreading their humanitarian service throughout Britain and to far-flung places abroad". The unit was open to anybody who shared basic Quaker beliefs that war is inconsistent with the spirit and teaching of Jesus and that the individual should be active in the task of reconciliation between individuals, groups and nations.

Because of my age, I happened to be one of the first to appear before a "tribunal" (itself perhaps rather confused about its function) in 1939. The experience convinced me that no tribunal, nor any person, can truly decide whether another individual's reasoning and decision is conscientious or not. I was brought up in a Church of England home, but with an unusually strong pacifist background. I soon heard about the Friends' Ambulance Unit and decided that I would rather work with them than do nothing or perhaps go to prison. Over five years, I found myself in the East End of London during the blitz, spending a year each in China and in India, and, after the war ended in the West, among the displaced Poles of north Germany. I am not proud of what I did during the war, but I do not regret it. Four of my friends later decided they had made a mistake and joined the forces.

Since 1945, ironically due to the atom bomb, there have been sixty years of peace between the major powers, leading dangerously to there being only one superpower. Yet wars continue, most recently in Iraq, and weapons become ever more deadly and destructive. The need for Quaker pacifism and its clear expression remains ever more urgent. Yet, though Friends sometimes seem curiously reluctant to emphasise or even discuss the peace testimony in public, pacifism is an essential and central part of Quakerism. In it, the sacred and the secular come more closely together than almost anywhere else.

For me, the Holy Spirit, the conscience and George Fox's idea of Truth are almost three expressions of the same belief, based on experience. The letters C.O. should stand for conscientious obedience – obedience to conscience – rather than conscientious objection. Each of us must follow the promptings of his or her own conscience.

3

I come from a long line of good people who never questioned the use of violence or the necessity of going to war. Maybe it was because my father died when I was four that I questioned this. I believed, from an early age, that life was something we could not restore – hence should not take. Once I went to Sunday School and discovered the Ten Commandments and Jesus' words about loving our enemies I was confirmed as an earnest five-year-old pacifist, withdrawing my support from all violence and violent structures. I recall a tinge of sadness that there was no more conscription, so I was unlikely to be a public conscientious objector!

As I grew up I realised that it wasn't (all) about passivity and withdrawal. It had to be about action to prevent things happening. So off I went on CND marches and anti-Vietnam War demos. I was troubled by so much of the violence on the edges of these and worked to try to make them more peaceful. (A wonderful toolbox of "nonviolent action" has been, and is being, built up by people all over the world and I wish I had known and understood more about this years ago.)

Then I saw that prevention wasn't (just) about protest. Nonviolence (in the peace movement this is a non-hyphenated word to emphasise its positive nature) includes building good relations between people, helping them to deal with their conflicts creatively. It must include working with those who are disadvantaged, addressing the injustices that lead to conflicts and then building the institutions locally, nationally and internationally which make for peace. That's not an idealistic, impossible agenda. Most of us are able to engage where we are as local people, in the work place and nationally when opportunity arises. Sometimes I still find myself in a situation where passive non-cooperation seems the right thing; at other times I hope I have been able to contribute to moving things forward creatively.

Quakers have never been very exercised by the hypothetical. I don't spend much time thinking "What would I do if..." I believe I act well by conscious preparation – and that includes my worship, prayer and learning about peace and nonviolence. My Quakerism helps me hold a vision in front of me of a nonviolent world. This is not easy. I never argue that nonviolence always "works" in the short term, only that I can act no other way. So it offers me a community of support, not least because it reminds me that I don't have to be active on every issue all the time. I can do what I can, where I can, as best I can and feel connected to others acting in their own way.

I have grown into an understanding that peace is not conflict free. *Life* is not conflict free. Learning how to handle conflict is one of the ways we grow to maturity. It is *how* we handle it that matters. The means must mirror the end we seek – so they must be just, healing and transforming.

Above all, I believe passionately that evil cannot be overcome by using its own methods, or by destroying the individuals involved in it. It needs to be confronted and transformed. The cycles of violence have to be stopped. There are no exceptions. I have to live as though that is always true – and I cannot do that in my own strength alone.

4

I don't like the word "pacifism" very much. Could it be that my slightly negative feeling comes simply from its similarity to the word "passive"?

I haven't been a pacifist all my life. In fact, when I first started to attend Quaker meetings, I found the peace testimony quite a stumbling block. I could understand the emotional longing for an end to war, but it seemed logical to me that military force was sometimes needed in desperate circumstances.

I understand now that I was making a connection which is entirely false. I thought that if people have a just cause, any war that they wage will, more or less by definition, be a just one. In time, I learned to pull this connection apart. I began slowly to understand that, while there may be many just causes, it absolutely does not follow that there is ever such a thing as a just war.

I have been very disturbed to read how passionately this idea of the just war is defended in Christian literature. St. Augustine and St. Thomas Aquinas, for example, both argued that it is right to use evil methods if your aim is the avoidance of evil. It's an utterly fatuous idea, but for some reason its absurdity seems to be lost on a lot of us. It was certainly lost on me.

I now look back on my old ideas with some disbelief. I find myself to be passionately opposed to all military action, for whatever reason. I'm too young to have been called up, but I am confident that had I lived through any of the wars I know about, I would have been, for religious reasons, a conscientious objector.

"The Christian ideal has not been tried and left wanting. It has been found difficult; and left untried." G.K. Chesterton wrote that in 1910, and during the hundred or so years since, nothing has changed. "Difficult" concepts (thou shalt not kill; love your enemies; do good to those who hate you) become impossible in times of war and are conveniently forgotten.

The misery suffered by people in the firing line is well documented: we all know about the indescribable horrors of armed conflict. But so long as they have what Thomas Aquinas called "a rightful intention", good people still justify the deliberate murder of others. Perhaps it's sensible to remember how rarely, if ever, those rightful intentions have been realised, how often and how subtly they are corrupted. For example, in 1939 well-intentioned, reasonable people declared war on Germany in order to liberate Poland. And in 1945 they bombed Hiroshima.

And if wars were ever proved to solve problems, what then? Well, if I base my life on my religion, I have to value that more than pure practicality. So I need to start at the other end and look at it from a religious perspective. And as soon as I do that, I discover a truth which, as far as I am concerned, cancels out everything else. It is this: nobody can take part in a war without showing contempt for the transforming power of God's love. This is absolutely crucial, it seems to me, because – and here I'm back with G.K. Chesterton again – trusting that power has quite simply never been tried.

It astonishes me that people who have found their personal lives changed and renewed by their relationship with God should be so keen to ditch the experience as soon as the crisis is a national one. Solving problems by seizing control never works. Yet we do it again and again, expecting different results.

And what should I do? Well, what I mustn't do is sit around and wait for other people to do the dirty work. It is essential to take the "passive" out of "pacifism" and the only way to stop a thing is to stop it. The first step must be to live a peace-based, nonviolent life myself. That means putting these principles into practice at home, every day, all the time. It also means doing all I can to support projects which explore alternatives to violence and conflict resolution. I believe that peacemaking is a skill. It can be learned.

The world will learn peace in the end. Sadly, I think it may take many hundreds of years, but I am confident that, in the future, nations will use the money once spent on defence to pioneer ways of resolving conflict. It is essential that this happens, because real global change will not take place until it does. We must march; we must agitate; we must argue. We must do everything we can to promote peacemaking as a way. This is not idealism, because it starts with us.

5

My first reading of the Quaker approach to peace was revelatory. It put into words the very position I had arrived at. That was how I wanted to live. I could aspire to such a way of life. In spite of my many subsequent failings, I still try, and have remained as convinced as ever that for me this is the right way. It is not easy. There are many questions for which I have not an easy or ready answer and I have learned to live with the comforts and the discomforts of my conviction. What I do know is that I do not wish to be violent or aggressive towards others, nor do I wish others to act aggressively or violently on my behalf.

My journey came about like this.

During the 1939-45 war I was at school and many of my family and friends were serving in the forces. It soon became apparent that war was not about deeds of valour and the glamour of uniforms. From time to time the commandment I had learnt in childhood, "Thou shalt not kill", would arise in my mind. This was church teaching, yet all the churches I knew at that time seemed in support of war. Somehow "we" were on the side of right. I do remember the powerful recognition that, just as we prayed to God for victory and deliverance, so did the German people; and just as the chaplains on our side blessed the men before battle, so did the other side.

With the ending of the war in Europe came the revelations about the carefully planned and executed extermination of so many people by the Nazi regime. I saw news footage of the death camps recorded as Allied forces advanced. The profound experience of this on a seventeen year old has lived with me ever since, and as I write I feel the same cold horror. Over the following years, many awful aspects of that war were exposed, including the suffering of so many under the Japanese military regime – not to mention the dreadful bombing of Europe by the Allies. The use of the atom bomb which ended the war in the Pacific numbed me, and I still hear my mother's words spoken in response to the accounts of the devastation wrought by the atomic bombs that fell on Nagasaki and Hiroshima: "There will never be another war."

So the years went on. Gradually the church I had grown up with ceased to have relevance. However, its Christian teaching, particularly the second great commandment to love one another, stayed with me. In my early thirties, I found myself on a spiritual search and to my everlasting gratitude was led to Quakers and read the great testimonies. It was, as I have said, as though everything came tumbling into place. The peace testimony cast light on where my experiences and thinking had led me. I was so aware of the sufferings of war. There must be other ways than war of settling differences. There must be other ways of sharing our human experience. I knew then that I could not answer all the questions that arise, such as "What would you do if ...?" and "What about Hitler and his attempt to execute all the Jews, the homosexuals, the mentally ill, the gypsies?" Later, I met a relative who had been a conscientious objector in the 1939-45 war, and he gave me great help. His brother lived in a psychiatric hospital because of injuries received in the 1914-18 war, and indeed died there in the early 1970s. The simplicity of his answer, "I did not want to do to anyone what had been done to my brother," put into words what has remained a truth for me.

I know how frail I am. I know I can react with an immediacy, especially in defence of another. Would I be able to do it with care and with love? I do not know. What I do know is that peace begins in the way I live in relation to all those around me. For me, as for many, there are no big stories to tell of having done anything of great note. I have not been confronted with major situations which demanded of me a really deliberate act of conscience. I constantly ask myself about such matters as the use of my taxes for war purposes. I am a very ordinary citizen, and I live in a society and a world where I am continually reminded of the almost unbelievable inhumanity which we as human beings wreak upon one another. I know that world economics place me in a very privileged position.

At the same time, I am reminded of the loving acts of human beings towards one another and the world in which we live, and I know that we are all one with another. I want to be able to live my life in accord with loving God and my neighbour as myself. In trying to live "in the virtue of that life and power that takes away the occasion of all wars" I know that I have to be constantly vigilant. I know that I frequently find my behaviour wanting. I know that I have no answers to many questions I am asked, nor indeed those I ask myself. Taking a positive position on peace is accepting that I must be active. It is not opting out. It is being in there. It is doing whatever I am capable of doing. It is owning up and saying, "I do not know," and it is saying, "I am engaged in the process."

6

I agree that pacifism may well be an ideal, but I have too many questions. What would I do if I were living in the middle of a conflict zone? What would I do if I had seen my friends and/or family being killed in brutal and unjust circumstances? Or what if I heard of Nazi atrocities and felt that an unstoppable evil was threatening my way of life or existence?

The answer is, of course, that I don't know. I live in a time when I am fortunate not to have to really answer these questions; we do not have conscription; thankfully, we do not have to contemplate a fight for survival of our way of life as many believed in the last two world wars. (Whether they were mistaken in their belief is another debate. Many Quakers and others did not so believe and refused to fight and accepted the consequences, becoming social outcasts and victims of the judicial system then in place.)

In another sense, too, this is all "too big" for me to use in a practical sense. Yes, I can write letters and attend demonstrations against arms sales and against illegal wars such as the one in Iraq. I can debate the rights and wrongs of pacifism too, but it is unlikely that I will really have to make the decision.

For me it is much more relevant and somehow "do-able" to begin with everyday life and everyday concerns. I can begin with *Advices & Queries*. I can try hard to respond to their questions and provocations in my daily life.

Advice number 31 asks us to "Search out whatever in your own way of life may contain the seeds of war," but for me it is the next Advice, number 32, that really is a help and guide. "Bring into God's light those emotions, attitudes and prejudices in yourself which lie at the root of destructive conflict... In what ways are you involved in the work of reconciliation between individuals, groups and nations?"

I think that what I am trying to say is that "peace begins at home", or rather peace begins with you and me. Reading *Advices & Queries*, we are repeatedly called on to be thoughtful, questioning, respectful of others and to value others' opinions.

So, what does that mean? Do I live a saintly life, devoid of conflict and malice? Of course not. What it means is that I try in difficult situations to think better of people and their motives than my initial feelings might lead me. I try to be less judgemental; I try to "take a step back" as pop psychology might say. I am successful and unsuccessful to varying degrees. I get angry and have rages and mutter words of criticism and condemnation, *usually to myself*, and I try to avoid using anger and argument to find ways forward.

In my work, I am a union representative and also a school governor. In both contexts there have been, quite recently, controversies and disagreements. At work, there is "restructuring", causing great anxiety and anger for many. I have found myself adopting Quaker principles in meetings: listening to people's comments, questions, feelings, anger, and reflecting back to them a "sense of the meeting" just as we would in our Meetings for Worship for Business. Rather than "going into battle" I have stuck to debate, argument and persuasion to achieve a fair compromise – involvement and influence in the process.

At the school of which I am governor, a relatively small matter became a great source of conflict and resentment. I remember asking for a period of quiet for us to consider what to do next. We did have some quiet and a way forward was found, where listening to each other was the key, rather than exchanging and repeating firmly held views in the usual adversarial manner.

A further help comes from Advice 17, which asks us whether we "respect that of God in everyone" and ends with the words "Avoid hurtful criticism and provocative language. Do not allow the strength of your convictions to betray you into making statements or allegations that are unfair or untrue. Think it possible that you may be mistaken."

This is what I try to do. Sometimes I fail; sometimes I succeed. For me the working for peace – or pacifism – comes in the trying, and the *keeping* trying.

7

At the first Quaker meeting I ever attended a Friend gave ministry to celebrate the recent abolition of the death penalty. She spoke of the hundred-year struggle by countless Quakers to help bring this about. From that moment I knew I had fallen among friends. For I had long believed that killings by the State through capital punishment were ethically wrong when human justice was so fallible.

That was the mid-1960s, and today I still worship in awe and admiration of those Friends who continue in the struggle to witness to the sanctity of life. For I have now learned what it means, in life-lived terms, for there to be that of God in everyone and that all of life is sacred. I join with those whose vision of life is sacramental, who know that to extinguish a human life or to damage the planet unnecessarily is an act of sacrilege to the whole and to the holiness of life: a diminution of the Spirit.

If I had become a Friend earlier I would also have known that my call-up for two years' National Service would have confronted me with three stark choices. Friends could serve with the armed forces if they felt the war was just; they might join the Friends Ambulance Unit or other relief work to proclaim the injustice of the war but identify with those suffering it; or they could feel called to take up an absolutist position and face imprisonment for the sake of conscience.

Quakers, having a testimony against all dogma, do not prescribe which of the three choices to make. There is only a compulsion to choose with profound discernment, not a compulsion to pacifism, even if that is deeply ingrained in the texture of the Quaker tradition from its origins. It means, however, that whichever choice is made, the Friend inevitably feels guilty about the other roads not taken. Reconciliation at the end of any international conflict has not always been easy among those who have taken the different paths. It is thought that about a third of the eligible young Friends called up fought in the Second World War, and it was natural that divisions in many Meetings were considerable when they returned, needing long and careful healing.

No one is a pacifist until they have been put to the test, whether in war-time or peace-time. It is a badge that can only be worn after the event. The times are always crying out for those rarest of prophets who can witness powerfully and symbolically to clog up the processes of the war machine and provoke the conscience of the multitude. I have so far failed the test but there is yet time.

Meanwhile, I have been moved to join with the peacemakers. Several of us some years ago initiated Leap Confronting Conflict, now the lead training organisation within the British Youth Service for conflict resolution and peer group mediation. I have also written songs and musicals and oratorios that told peace stories or celebrated the peaceable way, and I have attempted to live this myself. But I have become too entangled and encumbered to take a pure and clear stand as a pacifist. This needs a less worldly and more spiritual disposition. Quakers at large seem to be in much the same state. As a Society we challenged the immoral and illegal recent war in Iraq only in the ways of the "bourgeois pacifist", courteous demonstrations and polite newspaper letters. The Quaker termites of peace nibbled only imperceptibly at the foundations of power. Our latter-day respectability, economic prudence and lack of youthful vision increasingly hold us back.

As a father, grandfather and Quaker I know what it is to be in that same cleft stick, torn two ways. One, wanting my family to be safe; the other, knowing that all violence begets violence and is a spiritual blasphemy. My heart opposes all war and knows that nuclear war is genocide, an indictable crime against humanity. My head agrees to an armed police force in dire necessity, and to an armed peace-keeping force when aid is being distributed to otherwise starving refugees – both forces needing to be increasingly peace trained. Like others I must live the contradictions and help in the realistic planning of a better world, seeking inspiration to do so from today's occasional prophets of God.

This realism teaches me that it is in the minds of men that neighbourhood disputes begin, which the cornucopia of mediation and conflict resolution skills that Quakers have initiated over 350 years can increasingly address. But it is in the minds of politicians that wars begin and here our techniques and energies need to be of a different order. We give inordinate power to our leaders and must hold it as axiomatic that all power corrupts and absolute power corrupts absolutely.

We see daily in footballer, pop star, multi-national executive, pope and prime minister how the inflation of god-like celebrity and authority corrodes. Only by curbing power through more open, transparent, uncorrupted democratic processes, whether the United Nations or European Union abroad or an elected second chamber and a more forthright Cabinet at home, can we avoid being at the mercy of the psychic sickness that unbridled power induces. Our quest in the twenty-first century is to find new ways of speaking peace to power so that "nation shall not lift up sword against nation, neither shall they learn war any more".

8

I have experienced at first hand fewer of the effects of war than many people. However, I've seen enough of the effects to convince me that it solves no more problems or eradicates no more evil than it creates. Conflicts have to be solved by negotiation in the end.

In this age, wars can be waged at distance with less risk to the aggressor; trade and commerce operate through global systems and information or disinformation networks are faster and more invasive. More and more commonly can enemies be created to satisfy greed for resources, power or territory, and the people's will for peace is not strong enough to understand or overcome their fear of the enemy, or the perpetrator who may be acting in their name.

I worry about the fact that at the same time we and our children are learning more about war and less about building peace. There is much more information – and indeed entertainment – based on war and the waging of it. The aftermath or the repair of the damage is so often left to the heart-rending, charity-inspiring lesser "film bites" about the consequences. I have never seen a film about the reconstruction of Coventry or Dresden or indeed of Japan after the two nuclear attacks. I suppose it would be less dramatic.

I wholeheartedly support our peace testimony, but on a personal level, although I have feared on a few occasions for my life or the lives of members of my family, I don't know what I would do if I stood with a weapon between them and an attacker. Even if I wanted to, I don't think I would be able to kill or wound – but I have never been tested.

I admire and revere those who dedicate their lives to the cause of peace, sometimes tragically making the ultimate sacrifice. Now I no longer have the courage and strength of my youth, I try to make peace in small ways. I am reminded to "look for ways to mediate" and I also believe in the old slogan: "If you want peace, work for social justice."

9

I was born after the Second World War, but grew up in the shadow of it. My mother is a Russian Jew, and her mother, grandmother and uncle were gassed in a concentration camp. The blight of that horror and my mother's survivor guilt loomed large in my childhood.

One day, as a small child, I watched the news on television – a novelty since we ourselves did not have television – and saw one man shooting another in the head. It was, I think, the first time such a thing had been shown on television (it might have been in the then Belgian Congo) and it caused a furore in the media. It certainly caused a storm in my heart, and the image is with me still. I do not now watch the news on television or violent films; I do not wish to see such images, to become desensitised to the horror, to allow the sanctity of human life to be dulled.

I have not lived through the experience of war, except at a distance, so I cannot say how I would behave if tested. But those childhood experiences made it clear to me both how unthinkable the killing of another human being is, and that the unthinkable happens. It happens daily, all over the world, and we have been responsible for it in recent years in the Falklands, in Afghanistan and in Iraq.

These wars have politicised me, have driven me to go on my first marches for peace, to write letters to my MP, and also to train as a facilitator for the Alternatives to Violence Project, to learn to cope with anger and conflict in my own life, and to enable others to do the same. Anger and conflict are part of the human condition; it is how we deal with them that defines us.

It is not conflict or even anger that is at the root of most violence, I believe, but the notion of "the other". Only by viewing someone as other, less than human, can people torture and kill each other. Such a process led "ordinary" Germans to behave as they did against the Jews, gypsies and homosexuals; it is the beginning of that process, I believe, that allows us to exclude asylum seekers, travellers and some homeless people from our own society, and enables us to ignore the unkindness and violence meted out to members of those communities on a daily basis. It has to stop.

For there is no "other"; we are all one, interconnected.

I cannot imagine killing another human being, and I can't ask someone else to do it for me. It may seem a naïve or simplistic thing to say, but to discuss the issue in a pragmatic way misses the point: it's not a practical matter, but a religious one. It's like entering into a rational argument about whether God exists – it's not a matter of logic; it's on a different plane.

A delightful young man of 6 foot 4 (not a Quaker) told me the other day that he had once performed a citizen's arrest. "The other bloke punched me on the nose," he said, "and he didn't believe it when I didn't punch him back, in fact didn't even have my hands up to protect myself. He didn't know what to do."

Pacifism in action: the strongest weapon.

10

I am a pacifist – depending how we define "pacifist"! If it means someone who has never even felt a twinge of temper but is beautifully tranquil and has solved the world's conflicts, well, I have failed. If a pacifist longs for peace, justice and forgiveness, but quarrels, yells, cries and keeps apologising, learns and tries again, then I can count myself a pacifist. As I understand the principle of the Quaker peace testimony, peace is a process where each one of us tries to live a life that shifts the balance towards peace, and therefore towards a just and respectful society. We never give up this divine ideal.

But surely when peaceful means fail, we do have to give up and use force? My observation and my experience tell me violence brings short-term benefits and long-term costs. My father and others of his age were heroes with medals from the Second World War: I admire their courage, loyalty and sense of duty, their willingness to give their lives for others. They also killed and destroyed, and I saw the alcoholism, the scarred and damaged bodies, the orphaned children, the constant grief of the widowed, the fears of the Cold War. Sixty years later, I can still trace the devastating economic effects of that war in too many countries.

I can't sort out Iraq or prevent the next war. The task facing me, as a pacifist, is much smaller: to listen to my three nephews in the army, to understand each one's own ideals and experience and skill and then – but only if it seems right – to offer them a different picture of how problems might be solved. To me, that is what "answering that of God" in them means – not just a heart-to-heart talk, but a soul-to-soul conversation, in which I am as open to change as they are.

I know I have faced the temptation to violence, and I have failed, struggled, learned. No Quaker parents have been perfectly peaceful with their children. I think many have managed not to hit theirs, but all will have been unfair, or sarcastic, or imperfect in some way at some time – of course. I didn't want to be the kind of parent who slapped, but I did not know how to respond more usefully when our children were impossibly, obstinately naughty. I did learn, and years later I know I have been forgiven. I am so proud to see how one is a trained mediator, a good one too, and the other is a trusted childminder. We can change the cycle of violence.

It's the same in the Quaker community. Most of the time the local Friends' meeting really is a loving, supportive, challenging, interesting and enjoyable place to be. Conflict is inevitable among humans, but can we deal with it constructively, or does it destroy us? The traditional Quaker way is to meet in worship, in a small or larger group, where we can trust each other enough to be honest with each other and with ourselves. Whether we know God as a reality, or find richness in a divine myth, I notice that we put aside our egoism. Then we can see the other people involved are people, like us, and peace becomes possible.

Pacifism is not for cowards; it demands the courage to give your life, maybe to live with ridicule, even to break the law. Refusing conscription into the armed forces used to mean being court-martialled or shot. Now, part of my taxes – perhaps half – finances military action and arms sales. I remember the Quaker annual meeting, when more than a thousand considered the request of some of our employees to divert that part of their PAYE tax to peaceful means, such as overseas development. Our *Advices & Queries* remind us: "If you feel impelled by strong conviction to break the law, search your conscience deeply. Ask your meeting for the prayerful support which will give you strength as a right way becomes clear." I could not support such an impractical idea, yet I had the extraordinary experience in that Meeting for Worship of realising that, in order to follow God with our vision for a peaceful world, we had to try. Over the next year, Quakers pushed the matter as far as the European Commission on Human Rights, forcing the question to be considered seriously. This was when I understood the power of an ideal – the power of God.

11

"Force may subdue, but love gains." William Penn, 1692

Isn't the struggle between people spiritual? That is, where the spirit that one person aspires to express is challenged by others living out a different spirit? Are not the outward manifestations of struggle (denial, deceit, challenge, violence, war) just the physical consequences of different dispositions to life? And just as these consequences are written in the histories of our families, communities and nations, do we not sense them in each other? Often we quickly get a sense of the spirit in which another is living from details such as the look in an eye or the way the person holds their body.

I chose to work with difficult adolescents, both to ease their discomfort and the discomfort they caused everyone else. On one occasion one of the girls in my project sent for her boyfriend, whom I had not met before, to beat me up. He came flying up the stairs to where I stood at the top, blocking his way. In three seconds we had come eyeball to eyeball and in an instant he saw no defence in my body, no risk of retaliation, no ill-intent in my eye, no "enemy" to fight in my face, no threat. It was literally disarming. Though I would not move, he could not hit me. In one sense, there was nothing to hit. From this and other occasions I learned that, when under personal threat, I could put faith in a calm, firm, positive attitude where I didn't have a violent response to hand. Providing I was recognised as another human being (not an enemy, or an object), I was not at risk. A genuine, positive nonviolent disposition can also be an effective defence.

I think our Quaker testimony to peace derives from our sense of how the Spirit calls us to be, in particular how we should approach others and how we should view ourselves. Our denial of war is one specific outcome of this. Quakers have seen that we are all one of another, and have sensed our connectivity at a deep level. We have seen that we are to be equally valued as potential witnesses to the Light, we are each to be equally respected.

So how does the Spirit call us to deal with adversaries, people who are working against our goals, our means, our values or who are threatening us personally? How are we to view conflict, particularly as we are commanded to love our neighbour as (much as) ourselves?

Positively! Conflict derives from our differences, and from these we are shown more of humanity than we can know in ourselves. From our differences we see that our perspective is not the only one, not necessarily the best one, and when combined with others' enables us to see more of Truth than we could see alone. Treating our differences positively, with openness and enquiry, while insisting on our equal right to have our emotions and opinions heard, transforms conflict by influencing our interaction with others.

Conflict also provides the greatest opportunities for personal transformation (as every dramatist knows). Not only do we have to develop understanding, empathy, humour and patience, and to learn to look for common ground and common gain, but we also have to learn to accept and respect our adversaries, however much we reject their behaviour, their views, or their intention.

Yet the Spirit calls for more than this. We are called to live in ways that bring out the very best in each other, that "answer" that of God in us all. When in conflict we would hope that might prompt responses of a different quality, ones that offer both parties openings for growth, reconciliation and forgiveness. Sometimes this is only made possible through our own suffering, where it affirms but resists the oppressor, such as when Gordon Wilson forgave the bombers as his daughter lay in the rubble of the Enniskillen bomb, or when Mandela grew in stature as he provided dignified, positive resistance from his cell in Robben Island.

12

When I first came to Quakers in the mid-1990s, the peace testimony did not trouble me. Gradually, though, the Quaker way changed my life. I started by volunteering overseas with VSO. They sent me to a small Balkan country where I encountered the reality of war and what it does to people.

I arrived in Macedonia just before the Kosovo war began. Soon the population of the town I was living in, a few miles from the Kosovan border, was tripled by refugees. I came to understand how refugees are no different from us, just people caught in the wrong place at the wrong time. I learnt the human cost of violence.

Being so close that I could watch the bombers overhead, I understood the old adage that truth is the first victim of war. While NATO denied using Macedonian airspace, my own eyes told me otherwise. I saw how television shapes images of war. One-off incidents were continually re-shown, giving my panicky parents the impression that I was in danger.

Later, and more positively, I observed the reconstruction effort in Kosovo, and the impact of humanitarian organisations and soldiers acting as peace-keepers. I developed the conviction that civilians have a vital role in peace-building, but they often need to co-operate with the military in the aftermath of violent conflicts.

Unfortunately, this was only the beginning of my hard lessons about violent conflict. In 2001 there was an inter-ethnic armed conflict in Macedonia itself. I was there myself for part of the time. My friends were caught up in it and on both sides. The town I knew was at the centre of it. I experienced shooting, panic, and fear. It was a shock to hear normally rational friends raving with fear and loathing for the other ethnic group. I have witnessed how the approach of war makes people take leave of their senses so that they can come to believe the impossible: that killing and destruction can somehow improve lives, security and human rights.

This experience brought the Quaker peace testimony alive for me. Since then I have been trying to discover what can be done to resolve or, better yet, to prevent violent conflict. I have found that what I learned in Macedonia and Kosovo was not unique but applies to most wars.

By worshipping often with Quakers I experience unity and equality with others, feeling the connections, the power and the love which exist within and between us. At best we are in touch with a quality of goodness which never leaves us and which counters the despair that human sufferings and failings also always exist. We share one planet and are of one race, the human race. It takes time, and much reflection and study, to hold on to the view that peaceful means must prevail eventually over war as a means of achieving justice.

Gandhi said: "There is no way to peace. Peace is the way." Perhaps those who cannot be pacifists because they think there might be occasions when there is no alternative to war focus too much on those exceptions. If it seems too radical to start with "no war", think about "not this war". Remember the occasions when responding to injustice without violence has worked. In recent years it has brought an end to the division of Europe, apartheid in South Africa, and regimes in the Ukraine and Georgia.

I reject the idea of a "just" war. Wars, by the very nature of the means they use, are never just. They may be fought, at least by some of the protagonists, to right injustice; but that does not make what is done in the war just. People, groups, warlords, nations will join in for their own purposes, while others spur the conflict on from the sidelines by selling arms to both sides.

I feel deeply that using violence to obtain human rights and democracy is a contradiction in terms. Human ends can never justify inhuman means.

My vision is of a world where any state that tried to use aggression against another would be faced by the united resistance of all other governments refusing to sell arms to it; refusing to supply intelligence; and using financial and other sanctions. Instead it would have positive ways to raise its grievances and be heard through international political, economic and legal institutions. Within states, ethnic groups and individuals would also have peaceful ways to raise their grievances because of the universal acceptance of human rights, and access to fair legal systems, officials and police.

Living the Quaker peace testimony is being on the way to peace. I am still on that journey but I am accompanied and supported by Friends in learning about and working out what I can do for peace. I'm not afraid to think about war now. I am more afraid of the consequences if people with concern for others do not face these issues. Can we leave the future of humanity and the planet to leaders who think the ends justify the means, who do not respect all people, or who see life as a struggle against mindlessly evil enemies who deserve to die?

> *How about writing something about pacifism?*

WHO IS JESUS?

To me Jesus is a window through to God,
a person who in terms of personality,
in a way that can be grasped by our finite minds,
shows what mercy, pity, peace are like in human life.

Ruth Fawell, 1987, *Quaker Faith & Practice*, 26.54

1

I once saw the face of Jesus in a dream: on a cloth, like the Turin shroud, a Semitic face of infinite seriousness and beauty. At the time I had no faith, and I do not now regard myself as a Christian, so the gift of that vision remains mysterious.

I am touched by Jesus as a figure, moved by his place as an outcast – illegitimate, born in poverty – and the startling nature of his teaching. To put those excluded by society first, to show tenderness to those most abhorred, to focus on forgiveness and on love: this is profoundly radical. I am touched too by the devoted lives of the first disciples – it is to that vision that early Quakers wished to return. I do not read the Bible now, but I imbibed the Jesus story in childhood; its moral code is a part of me and of our Western culture, however little we live by it.

When I came to Friends ten years ago, I had great difficulty with any reference to the Bible or Christianity. It is only recently, belatedly, that I have begun to understand another way of looking at the stories, and to recognise how beautiful they are, when interiorised rather than regarded as objective literal truth, and when apparent historical happenings – creation, resurrection – are viewed as ongoing processes, not as one-off events. The first ray of light came at Meeting for Worship one Easter Day when there was a good deal of ministry about "resurrection". As a concept, dying to be reborn, it is enormously powerful. It is part of a process for each of us: little deaths of the self that can lead to greater transformation.

The same approach can illumine the meaning of the incarnation. I do not regard Jesus as the only son of God; I don't think he regarded himself in that way; we are all the children of God; we all have the potential to realise the Godness in ourselves. The

Buddha, Nelson Mandela, Gandhi: I am not original in pointing out others in whom the Godness shines. That for me is the meaning of the incarnation, of Jesus, and, for that matter, of Krishna too. And incarnation implies that the material, the earth, the body, are important too: that religion that splits off from the carnal is mistaken.

I do not believe either that Jesus died to save us from our sins: that primitive notion of sacrifice does not seem in tune with the revelatory nature of his teaching. In fact "belief" has no part in what Jesus means to me. For me he is not part of God, nor a mediator for a divine being, but a sublime teacher and example.

How much is literal truth in the Jesus story seems to me irrelevant, as do the historical "facts": how, where, whether Jesus lived, about which there has been a lot of recent research. Reading some of the gospels not included in the Bible, particularly the Gospel of Thomas, gives us a deeper, mystic reading of Jesus and his message. What matters is what he stands for: the "myth" in its positive sense as an underlying truth, greater than any particularity. The Jesus myth is glorious, poetic, revolutionary, and profoundly moving. To base a life on the love and equality that he stands for: one can do no better.

2

Early in my life with Friends, I overheard a conversation between a Quaker and a newcomer. "Do Quakers believe that Jesus was the Son of God?" asked the enquirer. "Yes," answered the Friend; then he added with just the hint of a twinkle, "and so are you and so am I." It was one of those moments that convinced me I was in the right place.

Why did it chime so strongly with me? I think it goes back to my religious upbringing – I was raised as an Anglican, and I don't remember a time when I couldn't reel off by heart the Apostles' Creed: a statement that had me announcing regularly my belief in Jesus' conception through a spirit, his virgin birth, his descent into hell and finally his resurrection and ascent into heaven, from where he will assuredly judge us all.

When I was still quite young, I remember noticing something that struck me as illogical in all this. Why would Jesus judge us from his heavenly position at the right hand of God, I thought, when he had already told us so clearly that if we don't judge we won't be judged ourselves? Such doubts seemed to multiply weekly, and by the time I was in my late teens I felt rather angry that I was required to recite a creed which I considered to be more about ancient, abstract notions of Jesus than the revolution he created and the wisdom he taught.

I have no such anger today. I accept that some people have concepts of Jesus which I don't share but which they find helpful. For myself, I feel blessed that I'm freed from the constraints of an imposed belief system. It makes me better able to understand, appreciate and love what Jesus said and did and to compare it on equal terms with what I might read in, say, the *Tao Te Ching*, *The Upanishads* or the Old Testament.

When I'm being taught, it's important to me that everything fits together. If I open the Psalms, for example, I read in the twenty-third psalm that the Lord is my shepherd; when I turn the page and look at the twenty-fourth psalm, I'm told that he is the Lord strong and mighty in battle. Anyone who has ever read about the life of Jesus, on the other hand, knows that only one of those two ideas lines up with what he had to say; and we can be sure about it, because in the paragraphs that people often call the Sermon on the Mount, Jesus is absolutely clear and totally consistent. In reading him we acquire an instinctive understanding and appreciation of his personality, of his humanness. We feel simply that we know him. And if we know him, we are better able to use him as our guide.

There is a moment in Jesus' life that haunts me, and which I feel that I have absorbed at quite a discomforting level. It is recounted in three of the four gospels. In the garden of Gethsemane, before he is arrested, he tells his followers to stay where they are, because he wants to go and pray quietly on his own. He asks God to "take this cup from me", but then adds, "not my will but yours". When he returns, he finds his disciples asleep. "Could you not stay awake for one hour?" he asks. And in two of the gospels, he prays again and they fall asleep again – twice more – as if to emphasise the lassitude, inertia and grief which have beset the followers of Jesus.

It is a continual, nagging reminder to me, a symbol of the need to stand up, to be conscious and to make sure that the inside of me is always the same as the outside. And the lesson is made all the more powerful by being drawn from the real life of a man whose truth shines out despite the theology. You couldn't invent Jesus.

The man's life and his teaching fitted together. He didn't just tell us to love our enemies; he did it. When he told us to turn the other cheek, he demonstrated it. He didn't just say, he showed us in his life, that love is stronger than death. So if I'm to take proper notice of what he taught, I have to live it too. I have to be aware of what goes on around me. I have to be in the world without positioning myself – as I so often do – conveniently just beneath the radar. I have, in all senses, to stay awake, like he did. I spend my life pinching myself – am I sleeping now?

3

I came to a firm knowledge that Jesus is the Messiah when I came amongst British Quakers. This is strange, because anyone who spends any length of time amongst Friends will soon discover a strong resistance to the idea that Jesus is anything more than a great teacher.

I started my spiritual journey as a teenager amongst conservative Christians who were keen to assert a belief-based religion. In time I become troubled with the way they made salvation appear very easy for themselves and impossible for someone following any other faith. On becoming a student in London, I found a way out of this mindset, and started on a long and complicated search over the religious map. I immersed myself in Islam, Russian Orthodoxy, Zen Buddhism, but having only my restless intellect as a guide I made little headway along any of these paths. I didn't see it at the time, but religion served a similar function for me as drugs and alcohol do for some other people. I was looking for something that would make me a different person from the confused, unhappy individual I was at the time. In a burnt-out and rather miserable state I found myself in a Quaker meeting.

I soon encountered people who had made similar journeys, many trying to get away from hard-line Christianity, so I could sympathise with them, given my past experience. However, I could see that beneath the openness and tolerance there were strongly held opinions. I became increasingly troubled at people's unwillingness to see the difference between the essential goodness of Jesus and the distortions of subsequent generations of his followers. I was also becoming frustrated with a religion that seemed to be defining itself by what it was *not*: we don't have creeds, we don't have sacraments, we don't have priests.

On the brink of setting out again, I met two American Quaker ministers (some US Meetings do have pastors). One had been in the very liberal wing of east coast Quakerism, the other from a strongly evangelical Quaker group on the west coast. Both had made radical shifts in their lives, and the message they carried was entirely new to me. They spoke of a Christ who had come to end all religion (including "Christianity"), by teaching people directly. They spoke of the risen Christ Jesus as a light within *all* people, revealing the things that separated them from true peace. This was something I craved and my ears pricked up. But the stick of dynamite that lifted me out of comfortable detachment was the message that Jesus Christ is as present to us today as he was to the disciples two thousand years ago. This really threw me and I now describe this as a "shock of recognition".

I started to make a connection between the pushings and pullings, joys and frustrations, highs and lows that had taken place with myself as I read of the historical person of Jesus in the Bible. What he was doing in Palestine he was doing in me; troubling my conscience, driving the money changers out of the temple, bringing the dead back to life, forgiving the unforgivable. With this connection I started to see that Jesus is not just a great teacher amongst many others. If *just* a teacher he is a confusing and poor one, simply because no human can go away with those teachings and hope to fulfil them on their own. About this time I had become interested in the lives of early Quakers and here I saw people doing exactly as Jesus commanded: not returning violence with violence, receiving persecution as a blessing, treating all people equally, not acting deceitfully.

There seemed to be something superhuman in their behaviour, and it perplexed me until I started to see the divinity of Jesus Christ was being demonstrated in their own divinity. I started to pay some attention to the light within myself, and by obeying it I started to cease from some of my worst behaviours and attitudes. I felt I could speak with some conviction of Jesus' divinity, probably for the first time.

It was some time later that a much older Friend spoke to my still confused condition: "People fret about the divinity of Jesus, but the thing they're really struggling with is the humanity of God." I was once told by some Quakers, after a talk I gave about early Quakerism, that perfection is impossible. The cultural conditioning of our society strongly favours modesty and self-deprecation, but, at the end of the day, coming into God's kingdom and seeing it formed on earth is the very purpose of being a Quaker. We often say we are "only human". *Only* human?

4

My upbringing in a Scottish churchgoing family gave me some powerful transcendent experiences and a good biblical education. I was taught conventionally that Jesus was the "son of God and saviour of the world", but I also learned how the Jewish and Christian traditions and religious writings had developed, and came to see them as a record of one of the strands of evolving human religious consciousness. By the time I started questioning things like a "virgin birth" I had both sufficient knowledge to discover that the Hebrew word meant "young woman", and sufficient commitment to the teachings of the prophet Jesus of Nazareth not to disregard the entire story. At university I began to explore the ways of the wider Christian community.

Some years later I became a Quaker. The silence-based worship had become central to my life and I welcomed the freedom which the absence of formal creed and dogma provided. For many years I concentrated on the religion *of* Jesus rather than the religion *about* him. In the Student Christian Movement and later in other ecumenical groups I found many others, in many denominations, just like me – concentrating on his teaching about love and justice, about the value of all as children of God, and his pictures of an "upside-down world" where the last comes first. We learned about liberation theology and feminist theology, and were committed to working together for justice and peace worldwide. We may all have had different understandings about who exactly Jesus was, but we were united in the search for what we could learn from him about how we should live our lives. I have learned over time from the understandings of other religions too, but the Judaeo-Christian tradition is the one where my roots are and whose stories I am best equipped to unpack and comprehend.

To some extent I am still content to theorise as little as possible about Jesus and to let his life and death and teaching speak. Yet that is not enough. Language is a major tool for communication. I need to try to express, however inadequately, what I am coming to understand.

Though my sense of the Divine is in the infinite and inexplicable, I see in the life, teaching and death of Jesus a reflection of God which enables me to trust that I may also find God near and in the everyday. Hence I have become confident that not a sparrow falls to the ground but it is known and loved, that there is not a single human failing that is not redeemable, or a joy or grief that is not comprehended in the nature of God. I conclude that the nature of God is to offer us a creative part in the universe. This is a God of attachment to all people, to the earth and to justice, and that has huge political and social significance for the way I should lead my life. Above all, I find, in the words of Bonhoeffer, the German theologian, "the transcendental is not infinite and unattainable tasks, but the neighbour who is within reach in any situation". The God I encounter through Jesus tells me I shall meet God as much in my action as in my waiting or worship. The way is costly. The only power I may use is love.

The historical record about Jesus is scanty. Though his teaching, taken as a whole, is compelling, many parts of it can be found elsewhere. For centuries those who follow him have struggled to interpret why he evokes such a profound response. Saviour of the world? Son of God? *The* son of God or *a* son of God? I find these words too anthropomorphic. These are concepts which developed in the Western church. Metaphors which the Eastern church developed in the early centuries after Jesus are for me much more helpful. Some spoke of humanity absorbed into divinity. The "Word became flesh" not as *a man* but as *humanity*. Maximus, in the seventh century CE, talked of Jesus as someone transformed and transfigured by the Divine – representing what we could/would all become.

But in the end these are all still "just" words. Ultimately, Jesus is for me someone who opens a window into the nature of God and reveals both the light and the darkness, the power and the helplessness of the Divine. He enables me to recognise and value the Divine everywhere and in everyone. He points to ultimate truth which we recognise in the infinite space of silence.

5

I love the spirit in which Jesus lived. For me that spirit is divine, and all that is divine.

Jesus was a Jew, steeped in his own culture. Jews believed that God had a covenant with his people but that it had not been fulfilled due to their unfaithfulness. They believed, though, that the time would come when the people would be forgiven, the

Torah would be kept and God would reign – although there were different views as to how this would happen. Until then, acts of sacrifice were called for.

Somehow, Jesus found a deeper calling beyond the law, and came to believe that he could help bring about the longed-for new age. With awesome abilities as prophet, teacher and healer, he set about proclaiming that the time had come, the Kingdom of God was at hand. Without condemnation he challenged those he met to turn and follow his lead, become humble, and live in the spirit rather than by rules. He told the parable of the Good Samaritan to illustrate how people can get bound in their traditions and forget the foremost duty of love and compassion which even foreigners would show. If the people would live in this spirit, when the time came they, rather than the pious, rich and honoured, would be chosen. He proclaimed that God is spirit, and those that worship him must worship in spirit and in truth, and that worship, it is clear from his teaching, is primarily in how we live.

Perhaps even during his ministry, Jesus came to see that to bring the kingdom into people's hearts would require of him the ultimate sacrifice, but that if he could remain utterly true to this calling he might be the agent of change. I feel he was right and that he succeeded, but perhaps not in the way he expected.

It started with the disciples at Pentecost. There, I believe, the spirit that is holy became manifest with an unprecedented power. The disciples had kept on meeting, feverishly trying to make sense of all that happened and trying not to change. Suddenly a wave of love and devotion swept away their resistance as they allowed themselves to feel the full effect of his life. Sudden internal changes have happened to me, when I fell in love for example. Only afterwards did I realise I had been fighting that "letting go", that dramatic change, that intense fusion. But I have also had my own private Pentecost, a moment when my admiration for the life of Jesus was transformed by love.

That moment was so intense that the exact details are lost to me, and its effects can only be described in imagery. I too had been seeking to make sense both of my feelings, which had been growing stronger, and of my thoughts, which were not yet formulated, but I do not know what triggered the release of love. For the disciples, perhaps the trigger was a moment when they realised that his death had been a supreme act of love for God and humanity. Whatever mine was, I regret not having been more faithful to it. I have no excuses.

You will have noticed I describe these events not in terms of external actions but internal ones. Maybe people fall into two camps depending on whether or not they are disposed to believe in a God that acts upon the world like a perfect father, intervening with love and anger, punishing or rewarding the wayward child. From this viewpoint it is possible for God to become man, for the Holy Spirit to be sent to whomever, and for the sacrifice of Jesus to change man's relationship to God, as though a debt had been paid.

In my view, by living the spirit to the full, Jesus showed humanity its greatest potential; he lifted our horizon. His life points to human potentials we do not realise. He sets the standard and calls us to follow through inner transformation. To treat Jesus as both God and man detracts from the power of his example and reduces his ability to speak to me. His life is all the more awesome for being fully human.

The spirit in which Jesus lived, the spirit that is holy, calls for our love. Yet we continue to resist this energy which, like a fuel, ignites and fires, offering us the power and motivation for the finest expressions of love, such as forgiving and altruism. This energy seems intensely creative, pulling us all towards unity. In ways I cannot comprehend, it also seems to have influenced events in my life that were not within my control. Amongst Quakers and others this spirit is our reference point, our touchstone, a spirit whose authenticity is known inwardly, for it has the ring of truth.

6

Poor Jesus. Would he not be disturbed to see how his message has been interpreted in the Christian tradition that claims to be based on his life and teachings? He was the prophet and teacher, who, as far as we can tell from the meagre historic record left us, urged his followers to challenge the religious establishment, to break away from stultified rituals of religion, and to approach God freshly and humbly. Yet he has been fossilised into a system of beliefs and practices even more rigid and hierarchical than those he opposed. The Jewish rabbi has been transmogrified into God, and he himself worshipped. Jesus the Jew would have found this blasphemous in the extreme.

The Jesus of my youth was an incomprehensible mixture of irreconcilable qualities. On the one hand, he was a magical figure, born asexually, performing supernatural acts and finally flying off into the sky to a hidden world beyond the stars. On the other hand, he was a gentle, girlish figure, surrounded by pristinely white lambs, and loving of little children (as long as they were good). On the one hand, he was God; on the other, human. Mysteriously, he was complicit in his own hideous, tortured death in order to save me from sin. How baffling.

As with my understanding of God, my concept of Jesus needed to cast off its childish baggage to be meaningful to me. When, as an adult, I became aware of biblical textual criticism and the work of informed theologians, I was able, by understanding the process through which this Jesus myth had arisen, to focus on the power of Jesus' ministry rather than his birth or death. I accepted that there were over one hundred years of biblical scholarship of which I had been unaware, and I began to absorb its findings. I started to discover a Jesus in whom I could believe, and in whose teachings I could find a pattern by which to live.

So, what did I discover? Probably nothing more than most educated, interested people know. I learned that the New Testament is a collection of writings dating from the time of the early church, altered at various times, often of disputed authorship, and all reflecting the culture of their time and place. Even the earliest accounts of Jesus' life were written decades after his death, and the earliest extant manuscript copies date from centuries later. The books of our Bible are those that survived the struggle of conflicting theologies of the early Christian centuries. Alternative views were silenced, and mainly lost, although one of them, the Gospel of Thomas, has recently been discovered. Very little is known about the historic figure of Jesus of Nazareth. The stories of his miraculous birth and resurrection have pagan origins, perhaps for the purpose of making the early cult acceptable throughout the non-Judaic world. Those who try to find the trinity and the sacraments in the Bible engage in a very dubious search.

So, I returned to the scriptures with a fresh eye. Freed from its mythical surrounds, the teaching of Jesus takes on a new simplicity and power. I am taken with the powerful image of this man, obsessed by a hunger for God, wandering itinerant throughout Galilee, assembling a motley crew of disciples and preaching the radical truths that he had uncovered. This is not a "gentle Jesus meek and mild", but a charismatic, rough-hewn human being, driven and troubled, seeking to know God and to do God's will in the world.

He teaches in an oblique, veiled style, that of pithy aphorisms and parables, offering facets of interpretation that are relevant to my life today. He promises the possibility of an intimate relationship with God, a transforming experience of the Divine in my heart. He presents a strong ethical code, demanding that I love and care for others, especially the poor and those marginalised in society. He warns me against hypocrisy, superficiality and ostentation. He teaches me to love my enemy, to answer violence with peacefulness, to forgive, and to put my trust in God.

And lately I have found meaning in the divine Christ as well. When viewed as a metaphor, the resurrection is a powerful image of rebirth following destruction, of truth and love failing to be overcome by evil: an eternal presence of the spirit. This Christ, the eternal love and truth dwelling in our human hearts, which is in the historic Jesus yet also in all of us, is surely God by another name.

7

I like Jesus' humour, the witty stories from real life, with endings that can make me gasp or laugh. He must have been good company, great fun, like my grandmother, still a strong and influential presence, still loved and remembered decades after her death. His friend Luke told of a dinner party in the house of a prominent, socially influential person – I imagine the embroidered cloths, the well-chosen wine, the exquisitely prepared food, the music – and then in came a woman of bad reputation who washed his feet with her tears – probably a prostitute from nearby

King's Cross, one of those shivering women I see on dark streets, desperate to get money for their children or the next fix, or enslaved by traffickers. I imagine myself there in that room – am I a saintly disciple eager to follow, or perhaps Jesus' revered mother, or his beautiful sister supporting his mission, maybe that woman trusting that Jesus could help her change her life round? No, to my shock, I realise that I am one of the Pharisees' cronies, disgusted that Jesus would let a woman like that even touch him, forgetting we had omitted that duty of courteous hosts to a dusty traveller. My comfortable life is in its own way as damaging as the Pharisees'. Jesus' way of teaching is so simple – just walk into the story; see for yourself.

Jesus taught through relationships – people gathered round him, listened to him, trusted him to heal their illnesses. He looked at their lives, saw the truth in their faces, and yet gave them confidence to change. I know perfectly well that God – whatever one could possibly mean by something so infinitely unknowable, beyond any concept or hypothesis – is not a person, as we understand humanity. Moreover, I know there are many faiths, many spiritual paths to our ultimate values, many different teachers, not just Jesus. However, I am human, a person, not an abstraction, rooted in a Christian culture, and in relating to Jesus I see what otherwise I cannot even glimpse. It's paradoxical, but I like paradoxes and puzzles. I am content with reasonable uncertainty – I don't look for unreasonable certainty any more.

I didn't understand the jargon used about Jesus such as "salvation" or "resurrection", until I encountered depression over a long period. It was in the stillness of Meeting for Worship – I remember the precise place and date – when I came to the conclusion that I had to choose between life and death. If I really loved my family, if I took seriously the wisdom of those I admired, I had to choose life, however difficult or risky, rather than the delusional safety of suicide. I made a promise to myself and to God that day, never to make the destructive choice.

That's when I began to understand the promise of new life that the story of Jesus' resurrection brings. Destroying what I most cared for – that was what despair meant to me – not that nothing was important, but that some things became too important to cope with. Yet to Jesus, and to me too, certain principles and testimonies are worth dying for, worth living for. Coming back to life three days after political murder, after being nailed to a cross in the heat of the sun, is impossible – but something happened that changed lives two thousand years ago, and still does.

Whether Jesus is a scientific challenge, historical fact, poetry, symbol or just a fascinating story hardly matters: to me, there is a reality that throws light on my path. It is interesting and fun to read about the theological or scientific possibilities, but they don't transform my life. Or, as Margaret Fell, an early Quaker, put it in 1652, "We are all thieves, we have taken the Scriptures in words and know nothing of them in ourselves." I have a kind of lively internal conversation with Jesus that nudges me to see things differently. We share a similar sense of humour; I see his stories still happening all around me. Walking a path parallel to Jesus takes me to ever-deeper meaning and gives me the courage, for example, to take on a scarily heavy responsibility at work. I think I am just beginning to grasp what Isaac Penington, another early Quaker, meant by "the law of the spirit of life in Christ".

8

When I think about the roots of my values and deepest beliefs I see that they are inspired by Jesus. I learnt about him in a Baptist Sunday school. There was also, at that time, a great deal of

Christian teaching at my state school, including a daily assembly with hymns, readings and prayers, religious education lessons, and the history of the Reformation in the sixteenth century. Britain has a Christian heritage and I cannot escape it.

But in myself I have usually been more ambivalent. My father and his relatives were all Jewish. Even as a child I knew they were good people, and rejected claims that Christianity was the only right way if it excluded half my family and half of me. Tolerance became one of my most prized values.

As soon as I went away from home to university my church life just fell away. Twenty-five years of career, relationships and homemaking followed with scarcely any overt religious practice, although I still recognised that my ethics were based on what I had been taught about Jesus. Later, under constant pressure from my mother-in-law, who not only believed that her particular variant of the Christian faith was right but that it was her duty to save as many souls as possible, I was forced to re-assess my beliefs. Then, after I stumbled upon Quakers, I was able to contemplate Jesus again, overcoming the aversion that my mother-in-law had induced.

Quakers let me explore Jesus without making me say I believe in miracles, the virgin birth, or the bodily resurrection. I have read about how little we know of what Jesus actually said. Those who wrote down his sayings may have distorted them, while others selected what to include in the Bible to conform to the doctrines of the churches. A book that was left out, attributed to Thomas, was rediscovered in 1945. As one commentator has explained, the Gospel of Thomas radically differs in two respects from the gospels accepted by most churches. It talks about the kingdom as something present now within us, rather than to come in the future, and it has no sense that Jesus intended to found a religion with himself at the centre of it. The Gospel of Thomas teaches that Jesus is a teacher of the right way to live. His sayings are more significant than himself as an individual.

Early Quakers seemed to have reached this conclusion, without having the scholarship and newly-discovered materials now available, and it suits me well. A faith which is liberal, tolerant, non-violent, self-aware, committed to mending the world, trying the way of love rather than hate, seems as needed now as ever.

As a choral singer I have sung many beautiful settings of the Mass. They include words from the creeds which many churches require their followers to accept and recite. For example, one version says of Jesus:

> For us and for our salvation he came down from heaven, was incarnate from the Holy Spirit and the Virgin Mary and was made man. For our sake he was crucified under Pontius Pilate; he suffered death and was buried. On the third day he rose again ...

This text includes much of what I find difficult to accept about Christianity, especially the virgin birth and the resurrection, supernatural events that surround Jesus' life like a halo. The life and teaching of Jesus are omitted in the creed, which leaps straight from "made man" to "crucified". What is it about human nature which makes a cult of great teachers, so that it becomes enough to worship them, rather than to try to follow their example?

As fundamentalists of all faiths become ever more clamorous, I have found myself wanting to defend the Jesus who told us to love our neighbours and our enemies; not to pile up riches on earth; and to look for the kingdom of heaven existing within and around us always. Churches which promise a future heaven just for their believers should have no exclusive right to call themselves Christian.

So I find myself, in a way, back where I started, willing to acknowledge the importance of Jesus as a role model for me, but never wanting to thrust any particular religious belief upon others. I can be at home like this among Quakers.

9

For several years, when I was looking for a spiritual home, I kept away from Quakers because I had been told that you had to be a Christian to join. I was not, and am not, Christian, in that I do not believe that Jesus was uniquely divine. There are other aspects of traditional Christian belief that I cannot accept. The idea that a loving God made a universe in which humans evolved in a way which was inevitably leading to transgression against a moral code laid down by that same God; that this loving God would mete out horrible punishment in an afterlife; that to save the situation Jesus had to be turned into a blood sacrifice that would at least secure mercy for those who believed all this: these things just don't make sense to me. They seem to mix pagan ideas about propitiating often angry gods with the Jewish monotheistic tradition, and the combination is horrific.

My search, therefore, started outside Christianity, with the Friends of the Western Buddhist Order. In Buddhism I found great riches. One is the acceptance that there are many mysteries for which we just don't have answers. The more we discover about the physical universe, the more unimaginable it becomes. We have no idea of what links conscious experience to chemical and electrical events in the brain. So how can we possibly know what might be in the non-physical world? Perhaps we are as ignorant of that as my cat is of where his tinned tuna comes from.

There was, however, for me, something missing. In the aftermath of 9/11, the main Buddhist answer to personal distress at the direction of American and British policy was to seek inner peace through meditation. I had meanwhile discovered, by chance, that many Quakers are not Christian in the traditional sense, and I had started attending my local meeting. Here all the emphasis was on doing what one could, however limited: vigils, marching and campaigning in other ways. The importance Quakers attach to practical action, both in one's personal life and in the wider community, drew me to them, and I soon became a committed member.

The Quaker emphasis on action surely comes from the teaching of Jesus, as conveyed through the gospels, about the value of each individual and the need to care for others, to love one's neighbour as oneself. One great achievement of the early Quakers was perhaps to disentangle the basic teaching of Jesus from the doctrines which developed about Christ as divine, as a sacrificial victim, and as the Messiah who would return. His teaching, however hard to follow, seems to me to be of central importance in today's world, and I accept and respect the Quaker values that come from this source. But I still call myself an agnostic Quaker rather than a Christian one.

10

Jesus began to make sense to me when I fell among Friends. My discovery of the Quaker way was as close to finding a community living the Jesus way as I could have hoped. The more I experienced Friends trying to echo in our time something of the way the historic Jesus worshipped and witnessed in his, the more he inspired and provoked. Jesus, I learned, needs to be humanised in this way to make him real.

I came from a stimulating Congregational upbringing but had never found credible the literalist's notion of Jesus, the Christ, born of a virgin, becoming a miracle worker and son of God, to be ultimately resurrected bodily into heaven, vanquishing hell and atoning for humanity's sins forever. With Friends I discovered this was all later material added to the Jesus story to speak to the expectations of pagans and Hellenes. I felt confirmed in my belief that humanity is one evolved family, with no chosen people, and that the physical laws of the universe are immutable, with no divine interventions – even in the face of genocide, holocaust or ecological extinction. I have become a Quaker following Jesus, not a Christian following the church.

I learned that Jesus was born naturally, perhaps illegitimately, not necessarily the eldest of a large illiterate lowest-class peasant family. He grew up in Nazareth, a small hamlet in the cosmopolitan and multicultural state of Galilee, under aggressive Roman occupation. But like George Fox, one of the founders of the Quaker way, he became a gleaner of ideas and insights from others and was early convinced that storytelling is the most unforgettable way of speaking to our deepest selves. His short time of public witness was mainly spent telling stories, in the form of parables studded with aphorisms, or engaging in dramatic encounters. These became burning tracers, barbs to hook into the memory and consciousness of the peasant audiences he urged to listen.

Initially he had followed John the Baptist's apocalyptic wilderness prophesying of God's ultimate liberation for the Jews from imperial bondage. With John's execution came new destinations. Freedom for the broken-spirited and dis-eased of heart had to be in the present, in the living now, not in some remote utopian future, and it had to be brought by those who had already been healed of their inner ills and alienation: it needed an infectious human power of hope and love. He became an exorcist of despair and rejection, an itinerant teacher, a sage and natural healer, so that all who were touched deeply by him found their lives transformed. He sparked a movement of wounded healers, sent out in pairs, to help re-kindle damaged spirits into new life. Jesus is humanity's epitome of a holy man: a spirit being. His genius sensitivities were open to spiritual healing, as Shakespeare's were to drama and Mozart's to music.

Jesus' enemies were those who caged the spirit: the self-righteous, the hypocritical, the proud and those who lived by the letter of religious text. His challenges were earthy not ethereal, leading him to realise that the Jewish way must be reformed and universalised. His vision was to proclaim the rule of God. This was not to be a kingdom or republic idealised in a heavenly realm for tomorrow but a state of the heart today, a condition of inward being, where acceptance, belonging and belovedness can be found. It was to be real, here on earth, for the poor and dispossessed, the lonely and marginalised, for women as well as men, for sinners, prostitutes and tax collectors.

This all-too-human Jesus gained his insights and leadings as Quakers would today, by withdrawing for brief periods from everyday clamour to take spiritual time away, finding a stillness through silence in which he could plumb the depths of his inner wisdom, creativity and healing: to wait in the light of the spirit within. Probing his own life experiences, he was led by promptings of love and liberation to explore how the divine way might come universally. It was to be based on absolute equality in the eyes of God; it would only come through the paths of peace and non-violence; it must be founded on truth and integrity; it was to be simple and accessible. The Sermon on the Mount and the Beatitudes say it all.

Quakers have based their testimonies and their lives on these great insights of Jesus. It was what I was drawn to in the historic witness of George Fox, John Woolman and Elizabeth Fry when dramatising their stories, and it is also what has inspired me in the lives of my contemporaries: Mahatma Gandhi, Nelson Mandela and the Dalai Lama. For I now see the "Christ" as a universal, the divine source within us all of compassion, liberation and creativity. This profound power is archetypal and makes us each a potential kindler of the spirit, just as we are each a divine child and an agency of resurrection. It is a way I want the courage to follow.

11

I heard stories about Jesus from a very early age, growing up as I did in a traditional Anglican home, and my first significant conscious memory is having asked a question of my mother about God and Jesus. Her reply was to the effect that they were spirit and were everywhere. Fast forward about ten years to hearing a vicar preaching a sermon on the trinity. His version was something to do with a three-sided lamp in which God was both central, and one of the sides. Of course Jesus and the Holy Spirit were the other two. God's light it seemed could come from all three ways. Well, what did a logical child do with that? If God was central why bother with the other two! As I stumbled my way along, this question seemed more and more relevant, and the church's attempts at educating me in such matters made little difference.

Over the years I increasingly thought for myself. The outcome was that I could no longer accept certain parts of the story I had been told concerning Jesus. The miraculous birth and resurrection, although wonderful stories, were stumbling points for me, and I could not respect a teaching which required me to recognise them as the truth when I could neither accept nor believe them. They may have been good stories, but they had no spiritual significance for me. The sacraments, too, ceased to have significance. Later I was to find the Quaker approach of trying to make the whole of life sacramental truly satisfying. For some years I blundered on, mistakenly thinking that this was what religion was about, and so rejecting it.

Then came a challenge when I was invited to go to church with a friend, and I reacted by deciding to read the Bible again. At first not very systematically, but then I made a decision that was to prove very important. I would read the New Testament and take what I understood. If something didn't make sense, I would pass on. I realised of course that the gospels were only other people's accounts of what they had heard. Jesus had not written them. As well, they had been translated from the original languages and had been written many, many years ago in lands and cultures with which I was totally unfamiliar. Witnesses too, I knew, were given to rendering surprisingly individual accounts of past events, and all of this seemed obvious to me when I re-read the gospels.

Today scholarship continues to be divided on this and much more. Of course, the four gospels tell different stories, but in my reading I realised that there was much that applied to my life. There were universal truths embedded here, and something much more. The Beatitudes and the Sermon on the Mount blazed with these truths. This light reached deep into me and set the direction I have haltingly tried to follow. I saw Jesus then, and still do, as a great Jewish teacher and totally human, subject to the same human frailties that we all are. What I have tried to follow has been that power of which he taught, and which so directed the little we know of his life.

No doubt there have been many who have been wonderful teachers. We know the names of some, and there are many more whose names we do not know. Some have left traditions with followers devoted to them, as in the case of Jesus. My experience of life, the culture I grew up in, its religious observances, its traditions, its arts, indeed its very language have all been highly influenced by the Christian tradition. Naturally, I see myself as coming from that tradition, but feel ambivalent about calling myself a Christian. I would rather say that I try to follow the teaching of Jesus. The notion of him dying for my sins has no meaning for me. The idea of all human beings being born into a state of sin I find, again, without substance for me. Nor do I hold with ideas of a divinity that selects only those who follow particular religious persuasions. What then, you might ask, have I left?

To this I answer that, as well the Beatitudes and the Sermon on the Mount, there is an underlying consistency in the accounts of Jesus we are given. This consistency is of a man who had a deep and abiding relationship with a loving God, who saw all humans as equal and free, and who taught that we are to love God and our neighbour as ourselves. Life lived so close to God, to the divine source, must be disciplined, yet so full and joyful.

12

We claim that the Quaker way is simple, radical, and relevant for today's spiritual seekers. Jesus too, in his time, preached of a spiritual path that was simple, radical and contemporary.

His key teaching was to love God with all your heart, mind, soul and strength, and your neighbour as yourself. This simple statement is complex: rich in its considerations and challenging in its practice. His message was relevant in his time to those who were seeking for meaning beyond the outward forms of religious practices. He dealt with issues of right relationships, of intent behind actions, of spiritual truths that were uncompromising. His radical ideas challenged the religious leaders and those who trusted in an outward form or authority for their religious status and security.

The accounts of his short public life describe a person who loved lively and robust company, including those who were on the edge of society. They were attracted to him and they sensed his compassionate acceptance of them. He was a man of integrity and he hated injustice. He sought times apart; he spoke in riddles; he hinted at mysteries; he made people laugh; he challenged hypocrisy; and some of his recorded sayings are obscure and hard to understand. At times he must have been a difficult person to be with!

So I reject all that presents Jesus, "the perfect man", as anaemic, fragile, with a simpering beatific aura. I abhor the representations in medieval western art which reflect church theology, for they diminish his spiritual leadership rather than enhance it.

The claim that Jesus is unique as the son of God, supported by the extraordinary circumstances of his birth, is not a hurdle for me. We are all children of God, each with the opportunity to become more whole, more in right relationship with the Divine. Jesus provides an example of what a perfect response might be. Nor are the recorded details of his death an issue of faith for me. It is likely that he challenged the authorities, religious and secular, and died the death of an agitator. That he should accept death as the inevitable consequence of the spiritual discipline he taught is what inspires me. If his resurrection means that the life force of Jesus, described as the Holy Spirit, is now accessible to us all, that it can be recognised, and bring us to a knowledge of and response to God, then I can fit this with my experience of divine promptings and guidance in my life.

But how do I respond to the claim that to be a true Christian I must accept Jesus as Christ and saviour? The language of sacrifice and redemption is difficult, and seems to belong to past cultures. Faith today cannot be based on a condition of unbearable guilt derived from dwelling upon the suffering of a crucifixion; pleading for mercy before the crucified Christ. The lesson for me is that Jesus showed how we can be opened to the possibilities of being transformed, of being recreated, made whole, arising from a sense of total acceptance.

George Fox, an early Quaker, said:

> Let the Light of Jesus Christ that shines in every one of your consciences search you thoroughly and it will let you clearly see. The same light which discovers the darkness also chases away the darkness...For the light has not only a property of enlightening but also of cleansing and sanctifying.

Then we see ourselves in dis-order, un-ease, not in harmony with life and love. And when we can acknowledge this then we are able to seek unity, healing and health.

There is limited historical evidence for the words of Jesus as recorded in the gospels, but their content, and the context in which the gospel writers set them, provide a wealth of matter for learning, spiritual insight and discernment. Those which bear the scrutiny of critical scholarship are a powerful record of Jesus' teachings and people's response to him. The passages in the Gospel of Thomas demand fresh thinking.

It must be accepted that the life of Jesus had a profound effect on those whom he met, and it must have been the quality of these relationships which were the basis for their faith in Jesus and in their living a new way of life. It is my Quaker experience that this direct revelation is continuous. It is one which has inspired me at different times in my life and goes on contributing to the small spiritual insights which change me, and my relationships with others and all creation.

> *Try writing 600 words on what you feel about Jesus*

HOW ARE WE EQUAL?

The soul is the image of God within you. Thus by
becoming aware of the soul, you see the image
of God in all other men and women – and you will
naturally behave towards them in a godly manner.

Meister Eckhart, *Talks of Instruction*

1

Equality is at the heart of the beliefs and values that I, as a Quaker, wish to live by. It is based on our central belief that God, and the ability to respond to and act in love and truth, is to be found in everyone. From that flows equality, in the sense of feeling respect for one another (and ourselves), listening to one another, and having the courage and confidence to speak our own truth, taking ourselves and every other person seriously, and recognising our common human needs.

Recently social science has shown us new and dramatic things about how people react to differences in wealth and power, and to equality and inequality. The first finding was that in each society rich and powerful people have less illness than poorer, and live many years longer. For example, in government offices in London the junior office workers have rates of heart disease four times higher than those of the most senior administrators.

As well as the statistical facts, we know *how* relative poverty leads to illness and death. The causes are not so much in the direct effects of people's physical circumstances -- a poorer diet or bad housing -- as in their minds. Stress -- caused by feeling powerless or looked down upon as a failure -- causes destructive changes in our physiology and body chemistry, starving our immune systems and upsetting our blood and circulation. And it tends to make us more violent and less co-operative.

In each society, poorer people have more stress hormones, more unhealthy blood fats, more arterial and heart disease, and worse immune function, than richer people. Again and again the pattern has been found -- less power, money and status: less health and happiness.

Those are the differences in health in one society. But comparing different societies gives a new insight. If we look at those countries whose average income is enough to avoid physical hardship and hunger we find that it is not the richest countries, but *the most equal* that are the healthiest. Hundreds of studies have shown huge differences in many kinds of physical and social health between countries such as Japan and Scandinavia – where income differences are smaller – and more unequal countries such as the USA and, increasingly, Britain.

It's not just life expectancy which is badly affected by greater inequality, but the incidence of many important illnesses. There is three times as much mental illness in less equal countries. The same pattern is seen in social ills – crime, the numbers of people in prison, the extent to which people say they distrust and fear one another, and in the ills that lie on the borderline between personal and social, including the incidence of teenage pregnancy, of suicide, obesity, drug and alcohol abuse and smoking. The differences show up even within one country; for example there are *huge* differences in homicide rates among states in the USA, from less than 10 per million people to about 170, correlating tightly with economic inequality.

In understanding how people feel and how it leads to stress, violence and so on, the key concept is "respect". A psychiatrist, working in American prisons, wrote: "I have yet to see a serious act of violence that was not provoked by the experience of feeling shamed and humiliated, disrespected and ridiculed." In modern unequal societies, poorer people feel like disrespected failures.

You know the pattern that I call "kicking the cat". In the stereo-typed story, the boss gives a man a bad time at work. He goes home and shouts at his wife. She cuffs the children, who kick the cat. All fairly trivial, at that level. But that is only a reminder of what research has shown – that in more hierarchical and unequal societies there is less equality of respect between men and women, more racism, and more domestic violence. People, particularly men, who feel humiliated and disrespected tend to turn on other individuals or groups where they can exert power or assert their superiority.

What do all these discoveries about equality mean for me? Firstly, they powerfully support my Quaker understanding of equality, not denying its spiritual aspects, but supporting them. They also tell us how we need to put it into practice, in every encounter with every person we meet. Quakers do that already, embodied in our equality in Meetings for Worship and for business, and the way we take turns at the many jobs and positions in the meeting.

We must take those values out to live them as individuals and communities. Friendship, in its ordinary sense, is also important; people with more friends live longer and with less illness and stress. They feel known and valued as themselves, as equals. And we must do all we can to get our governments to understand this new evidence, and make the changes that only they can. They are – rightly – worried about violence, crime, ill-health, over-use of alcohol and other drugs; but they seem not to realise that by reducing the inequalities of wealth and power in our countries they could make huge improvements in all these things at the same time, and in the happiness and well-being of all of us. We need to think how power and wealth, respect and esteem can be more equally shared, in every part of life; in political systems, in work, and in how we live together.

2

I was brought up to be special. I was a much-loved child, but it was more than that. The family considered itself special, somehow better than other families who were less educated, less intellectual, less, well, fortunate. There was a lot of compassion for people of differing abilities but they were not considered equals. There were strong demarcation lines in how we looked at gender, class, sexuality, disability and race. I was on the dominant side in every case except gender, and never suffered from that. It was a very sharply divided view of life.

I do, however, remember a strong sense of justice as a child and would often rebut racist comments – to the extent that my mother said I "had a thing about it" – and stood up for the bullied teacher, because I knew that she as a human being had the same sensibilities as the children who goaded her. And when I was twelve I refused to take up a scholarship to a boarding school, because I wanted to be at home and wanted to go to an "ordinary" school. I did not want to be posh.

Of course I moved away from that child's perspective, but preconceptions remained. When I came to Quakers, attitudes were challenged that I hardly realised I had. I found myself in a non-hierarchical community; a group of people who celebrated difference, and had in common values that were more important than what separated them. The divisions began to blur.

But it was the first time I went on a tea run for homeless people that I really woke up. I was nervous: sure that I would either be sneered at or hit over the head by a bottle-wielding druggie. That isn't what happened. Instead, as I walked over to a young man in a sleeping bag and asked if he would like a cup of tea or coffee, and whether he took sugar, I found myself forming a relationship with another human being. Instead of stepping over a bundle in a doorway with embarrassment and guilt, I was doing something, however small, and my preconceptions fell away. It was an epiphany, and has shaped much of the work I have done since.

That first experience and others that have followed it have affected my view of myself and how I relate to others. They peeled away a veneer of defensiveness to reveal a commonality I had not understood, and had not wanted to face.

For as a family we were also "special" in less comfortable ways. I was five when my father was diagnosed as a schizophrenic, and my world changed. After those five golden years, the uncertainty, embarrassment, responsibility, of my father's illness – as he obeyed his voices, talked to himself, accosted people in the street, emptied a suitcase full of banknotes into the gutter – took over the lives of my mother and myself. Friends and family deserted him; my mother – a Russian, a Jew, and never really accepted by my father's family – was a stranger in a foreign land. And I felt an outsider, never knowing where I fitted in. As a defence I accepted the status of being "special", took a pride in being different.

It's only as I've grown older that I have realised that many people feel that they don't belong, and maybe many bolster themselves, as we did, by feeling superior to those who are more visibly "different". I have come to recognise that the way society excludes some groups of people is not only a fear of the difference of others, it's a fear of their own difference. So, for me, working with the "outsiders" in society has been closer to home than others would know.

For the more I hear the stories of homeless people, of refugees or of prisoners, the more I know that it could have been my father, had my mother not looked after him for forty years. It could have been my alcoholic ex-husband. It could have been me. I now understand how completely we are one in our human predicament. *There is no other.*

But if we recognise the potential for disintegration in ourselves, the obverse is also true – and more important. The generosity shown by people who have least, the dignity of many suffering pain or injustice, show that no matter in what condition people live, no matter what misfortune has descended, or what mistakes have been made, the potential for achievement, for a good life, is there in everyone.

Equality does not mean I am not special. It means we all are.

3

In the introduction to the Quaker booklet called *Advices & Queries* we read, "The deeper realities of our faith are beyond precise formulation and our way of worship based on silent waiting testifies to this." It is a still, simple, quiet way of worshipping where all are seen to be of equal importance and none has any greater responsibility than another. Any present may find they are led to speak, usually briefly. We are all there in exactly the same relationship. We sit in a circle so that we can see one another's faces. No intermediary stands between us and the Truth. It is a way of worship that "allows God to teach and transform us", and generations of Quakers have been guided by the insights and testimonies which have come from it.

The testimony to equality has helped us see that the "light within" is the sole guide for each one of us. Each person, child or adult, is to be treated similarly. We try to have no regard to social status or any of those other criteria which come so easily to our minds, and can lead us to discriminate between people. We try not to judge them on their age, sexual orientation, skin colour, dress, the colour of their hair or lack of it, their education, or any other of the manifold criteria which our human minds can conceive.

When I first met Quakers, this basic philosophy was such a balm to my soul. I had long known that there was more than I had been able to find or to express. I knew that nothing I had found seemed quite right to me. Quaker worship was all the evidence I needed to recognise that much of what I had found for myself naturally followed, and the discipline which ensues was absolutely what I needed.

I was fortunate in that I was brought up in a home where care and concern for others were important. As a young child I had become aware of some of the social issues and injustices of the small mixed-race community in which I lived. However, there has been much for me to learn and I have been grateful for those who have helped me. I think of a contemporary in my teenage years who pointed out that certain language I was using was racist, or later of friends who took me into their confidence as to the way their skin colour meant they were treated.

Feeling embarrassed or condemning others, let alone railing at life's injustices, led nowhere. Very gradually I learnt to take responsibility, to look at myself, to try to be better informed. I found working professionally on equality of opportunity was testing. Challenged to develop a personal philosophy I arrived at the following: *Most people can do most things, even if we do them differently.*

Though for most of my life I have worked and lived in large cities, much of what I observe is a microcosm of that small community in which I grew up. The racism and the prejudice that we can all so easily be caught by is there in just as great a measure. We all need to be aware of it. When I find myself viewing someone in a negative way I am reminded that "we are all equal in the eyes of God". On the other hand, some forms of human behaviour can be overwhelmingly abhorrent to me. The only way I am able to deal with this is by leaving it to one side for a time. Subsequently, little by little, I try to view the person as my neighbour, to "meet" them in the tiniest of positive step-by-step moves, whilst trying to put away my desire to judge and condemn.

When I am being totally honest I see I am often far from leading my life without racism or prejudice. At such times I may feel frail and despairing. Will I never learn? Will I ever begin to understand? At these times I am helped by my Quaker discipline. *Advices & Queries* 32 begins, "Bring into God's light those emotions, attitudes and prejudices in yourself..." and almost always checks me. When I follow it through I find my awareness heightened and my resolve strengthened. It is as though I am accepted and able to go forward whilst knowing that my human frailties continue with me.

As I worship I am reminded again and again of that love which in its purity is the source. How do I keep this as a filter through which I view my world? I believe that the answer lies in the very reason that religious people through the ages have advised the practice of the constant presence of God. When I reflect on Jesus' teaching to love God and my neighbour as myself, I find my resolve strengthened. Today, in a culture which seemingly pays less and less attention to the teachings of the man we know as Jesus, I reflect that so much of his teaching was against being judgmental. Many of his followers seem to ignore this. It is in the stillness and quiet of what I call worship that I begin to understand that the power I find there is about a love that transcends all. A love that sees all of us as equal.

4

Experience, ideas and words give meaning to each other: I cannot remember which came first in my childish understanding, though I recall that tropical landscape vividly. We didn't use courtesy titles within our family -- affectionate nicknames or first names, but never "auntie", and we could tease, provided we were kind. Pushing my grandfather into our swimming pool was wrong, because of his frailty and arthritis, not his seniority. Locking our black maid into the laundry as a juvenile joke was an inexcusable conformity to the surrounding apartheid, a misuse of our parents' status as her employers, and led to the most serious punishment and talking-to ever. The less powerful a person, the more fair and courteous we should be.

The intense beauty of that country brought tears, an early spiritual experience. The Bible inspired me with declarations like "in the image of God, male and female, God created us". It seemed so obvious: we are all equal, but the Quaker *Advice* points out that "spiritual learning continues throughout life, and often in unexpected ways".

As I grew up, I encountered other inequalities – social class, immigration, unemployment. "Challenge" is a jargon word, but it does suggest that insights can come with conflict, and that giving up prejudice sometimes hurts. As a parent I learned that equality is not the same as uniformity. Our children have contrasting personalities, diverse gifts, varied needs: each is wonderfully unique. Of course I knew they were individuals, but didn't always remember how different. I grieve for the times we didn't manage the ideal combination of equal love and appropriate care, but am delighted and warmed that they love us anyway. They taught me humility and forgiveness, spiritual skills that I am still developing.

I thought I had sorted equality, but found my childhood insights needed updating. Why did I react with such deep hostility, as if by instinct, when in recent years women wearing the *niqab* appeared in this city? I had to dig back to my childhood, and untangle the assumptions of culture, race, religion and family habit. Black clothing was for widows, for death, and we needed bright colours after a world war. My family lived under military dictatorships, where a covered face indicated a guerrilla, or the police, both feared. At carnival, fantastic masks allowed people to ignore their normal personal or moral boundaries.

An open face, however, was a sign of honesty, so my father would brush my floppy hair aside, turn my face up and urge, "now, tell me the truth"; a hug would follow reconciliation. Jesus is recorded as seeing the Truth in people, especially those despised by society, and so healing and liberating them. Quakers have a testimony to truth: without that openness to each other, to learning, to our ideals, we cannot live equally, peacefully and simply. Now, when I see my neighbour with a veiled face, I remind myself that in her culture it is a sign of modesty and religious commitment, not intended as a barrier.

It takes time to change the ancient prejudices of childhood, because we don't always know how they developed. Furthermore, prejudices and assumptions interact. Courage and the skill of honesty are needed, if we are to follow fully Jesus' example of love.

When I developed one of the invisible disabilities I learned another painful lesson about inequality. A deaf friend said it was disappointing not to hear someone's joke and to have to ask for repetition, but a real rejection to be told, "Oh, don't bother, it wasn't very funny." It can be humiliating to have to ask for the "disabled" toilet if you look perfectly mobile, but you need to be able to wash. Mental ill-health can be particularly difficult, as it can *feel* to others as if the relationship has gone wrong. For example, someone depressed may behave as if she doesn't like her friends, when actually she is believing they couldn't possibly like her.

Black people count disproportionately in the mental health services in Britain, and the cause is surely a complicated mix of culture, inheritance, trauma, circumstance, prejudice and other people. Ignorance can distort diagnosis. If you hear God speak, are you deluded or a Quaker? Or maybe both?

I was horrified to discover that in some faiths, people whose bodies are perceived as "deformed" cannot enter the sanctuary of their place of worship, or participate in certain rituals. One friend of mine would not have a tattoo, as that "mutilation" would debar him from his religion's cemetery. I do dislike tattoos, but I cannot imagine that divine love would reject anyone so decorated! Barriers are caused by attitudes and ignorance, not by who or what we are.

Meetings for Worship are open to every person who is open to the Spirit. No one is perfect, we are all incomplete, unfinished humans. Instead, we come to worship to grow in wholeness. The only qualification is that we treat all the others equally, safely, as if they too were made in the image of God.

5

Quakers' central focus is on living in the Spirit, a spirit characterised by love. Whether it is in our lives, our worship, our organisational structures or deciding what we should do as a Society, we aim to discern and express that Spirit. We discern primarily through our inward sense of guidance, but also corporately and with reference to our collected wisdom.

It is central to Quaker faith that everyone can sense the guidance of the Spirit/Light/God if they give it attention. In this sense we see everyone as equal. What this means about how we should live – our spiritual contribution – is that we should see each other as unique, precious and children of God, and that we should give all others and ourselves equal respect. Quakers do not strive to make everyone equal, but in many fields where people are not given the respect they are due, Quakers are prominent in working for justice, for an end to violence, for universal education, prison reform and much else.

Respecting ourselves equally with others also means that we should each strive to become our full selves, while also enabling others to do the same. I have experienced the conflict in these objectives when making decisions about school places for my children, a second home, private health care, investments, air travel or the ways I spend my time and resources. To take this further, perhaps I should check if I am seeking my advantage at another's cost, or who is really paying for my standard of living.

Much of my work has been about relieving some of the negative outcomes of social and personal inequalities. The causes were various – a poor home life, low income, lack of perceived opportunity, homelessness, unemployment or being trapped in benefits. As my understanding of the suffering in others' lives increased I would look for ways to reduce it, and a series of projects ensued.

One was a scheme to help homeless people get accommodation in the private sector. There are financial barriers and negative perceptions on both sides which hinder this and we found ways to overcome all of these for over 1,200 people. We soon became aware of the dense overcrowding amongst refugees from the Horn of Africa countries, almost all Muslims, and set up a dedicated service which accounted for about forty per cent of all our tenancies.

Another project helped women caught in "the benefits trap" to start trading their way towards independence. Almost everyone choosing to participate was from an ethnic minority. With the support of a worker, small groups of women would meet regularly to work out what business each could run. When everyone agreed, a group member would take a low-cost loan to get started. We had researched how this system worked in Bangladesh and were delighted to find that our loans were also being repaid in full.

Supporting people and respecting them sometimes needs careful handling. Community furniture projects have people referred to them because they are unable to purchase commercially what they need. Each project has to decide whether to charge people for second-hand furniture or give it to them. If we gave the furniture away I felt we risked damaging their self-respect and reinforcing their ideas that they couldn't manage their own affairs. We developed a subtle process which aimed to get them to pay what they could afford.

I've encountered the same considerations, but magnified, when travelling in the Third World. How much should I tip a *tuk-tuk* driver in India, I wondered? He asks for two rupees, whereas a London taxi would cost two hundred or more. If I gave him much more than he asked it would help him immediately, but with time would it not help destroy something in him?

Gandhi advised that before taking actions we should consider their effect on the poorest people in society. Now, alongside many others, I am increasingly looking at how not to consume more than my share of the world's resources. My progress is slow on this journey but the imperative surrounds us. Our whole way of life is questioned by the huge inequalities of consumption. The goal of sustainable development may need to give way to seeking sustainable regression.

To go forward, we must look back to our roots. The future peace and security of much of the world may depend on more people treating each other with the respect due to another child of God. We must restate this conviction in ways that can be heard today. We must join with others. And we must live our lives in witness.

6

We are all children of one Source. There are no favourites, no chosen people. No one asks to be born. Every person is equally gifted with life and equally to be valued as an expression of it. Each of us is different, with unique DNA, but each is a member of one human family.

I wrote this when a young schoolteacher, challenged by the sixth form to write a "credible" religious play for them to perform in a local church, and I needed to clear my inner ground. The play became *Legion*, based on a healing story of Jesus in which a rejected, insane man is dramatically made whole again and integrated back into his community, his value restored.

Our setting was contemporary to bring home the needs of the mentally ill today for dignity and respect. It proved strong stuff. During rehearsals a sixth former lent me a book about Quakerism from her mother, who felt my beliefs seemed close to the Quaker way. Within two years I had become a Friend and was soon writing for their performing arts project, the Leaveners, exploring

Quaker concerns for peace and truth and equality.

In a musical play about George Fox, a seventeenth-century founder of Friends of Truth, as the Quakers were first known, we told the story from Worcester Gaol, during his seventh long imprisonment, of how as a young man he came to experience "the fire and hammer" of truth. Performed over a national tour by the Quaker Youth Theatre, itself a company which is open for anyone to join without audition or experience, we sang of his insight that "The Light shines through all" – so its mediation by professional clergy becomes unnecessary, for we are all its ministers.

Fox proclaimed we are equal in the eyes of God and must be equally treated on earth: this was treason in a class-ridden, aristocratic society. He saw there was "that of God in everyone". I have now come to see that every person is wholly made up of God-stuff, star-dust, energised by the Originating Power, the Creative Spirit, and that ours must be a sacramental vision. So to damage or kill, neglect or diminish another human being is sacrilege, an act of blasphemy. We are impelled to love our neighbours as ourselves: they are our equals. When Fox died, one in a hundred people of England was a Quaker. The play finishes in hope.

Later I worked with the Quaker Festival Orchestra and Chorus to present a full-length cantata exploring the witness of John Woolman, an eighteenth-century American, awakened in his youth to the evils of owning black slaves and appropriating Native American land. He saw the "Negro" and the "Indian" as our brothers, worshipping the same universal Spirit, for "God was not partial" to his children but loved them all. His was the first significant white voice to be heard denouncing the slave trade, and his task was to urge Quakers to put their own house in order.

Readings from his *Journal*, with songs based upon it, told of his journeyings to Quaker meetings throughout the New England states, encouraging Quaker landowners to see that owning slaves was debasing them, as well as treating human souls as beasts. In 1758 his Yearly Meeting in Philadelphia became the first to pledge an end to slave ownership, while his pamphlet-writing indirectly inspired Thomas Clarkson to begin working with Quakers campaigning throughout Britain. The slave trade was abolished in 1807, and we sang with passion at its bi-centennial celebrations.

Quakers were deeply troubled in the 1990s that their work for restorative justice in the penal service was increasingly thwarted by a Home Office concerned more with votes than rehabilitation. So in a musical play with the Quaker Youth Theatre I addressed Elizabeth Fry's life, an upper middle-class nineteenth-century Quaker currently featuring on our five pound notes, drawing on her spiritual diaries to give authenticity. A mother of thirteen children, Betsy lived in the heart of the city of London; she braved the sordid hell of nearby Newgate Prison to work with the ferocious women prisoners and their children.

She treated them as equal members of her own family, bringing them education, occupational training with earnings, care for those about to suffer deportation, "wholesome" open association in daytime and defended space from rapacious men at night-time. She recruited other Quaker women to work with her, encouraging such teams to develop around the country. Her insight was that prisons were not for social vengeance but could be places of change for those who "but for the grace of God might be me". We paralleled that understanding with the real story of another Norfolk-born Elizabeth, Lizzie, abused, poverty-stricken and ultimately hanged – a lifelong spur in Betsy's conscience.

Public performances about those who powerfully witness to

Truth draw on empathy from enactors and audience alike: they are seeds of time. We can rejoice that such Quaker visionaries have contributed to the growing international struggle for human rights and our national equal opportunities policies: for without social action spiritual insight is flummery. These secular compassionate expressions now shame the orthodoxies of most religions which dare not give dignity and respect due to women, to those of differing sexual orientation, even to those of other faiths. There are great struggles of inequality still to be endured that we shall have cause to celebrate in song and story.

7

By refusing to remove their hats or to bow before monarchs, aristocrats and judges in the seventeenth century, early Quakers were living out a revolutionary idea. I wonder whether, in the twenty-first century, with all the legislation against discrimination on the grounds of gender, race, religion, sexual orientation, disability and so on, the Quaker testimony to equality is still as radical.

Quakers do sit comfortably alongside secular, liberal reformers on what the law should be. Yet there is a profound difference arising from the way equality is rooted in our communal form of worship. Any group of Quakers can hold a Meeting for Worship at any time. There is no priestly hierarchy. Anyone present can sense the Spirit, which some might call God and others might not, and feel connected to it and, through it, to one another. Anyone, a Quaker or a first-time attender, young or old, man or woman, can speak if they feel they have a message that needs to be shared.

After several years among Quakers I have come to understand that the essence of equality is equal worth: worth that is measured not in money, but in humanity. Each of us, every single one with the possible exception of pregnant women, is only ever "one human", regardless of nationality or skin colour. The Quaker way challenges me to look for and respond with love to the "one human" in every encounter. While I find this impossible to achieve in practice, this ideal signposts for me the direction to follow.

As I follow the Quaker path, I have been shedding a mindset of hierarchy, learnt in the civil service, where promotion rather than a pay rise is used to motivate people. I remember the shock of realising for the first time, many years ago, that people in senior positions in government and business were human like me. They too might be feeling unwell or worried about family matters.

But was I just being offered access to an elite world? My self-assurance sometimes makes others deferential towards me, which in turn makes me uncomfortable, as it is undeserved. So many people accept hierarchies without question. They may never have been treated with respect themselves. Paradoxically, as much as I want to treat others as equals, sometimes they will not allow it, but place me on a pedestal. I have noticed this most when in poor, patriarchal societies, where I am treated not as a woman but as a Westerner, but it happens in Britain too, even within my own family and workplaces.

So I try hard as a volunteer working with refugees, to treat each asylum seeker who comes for help as a human being, not an alien, which is how the system sees them. But can I also bless everyone I work with, paid staff and volunteers, the officials I call on behalf of clients, the person serving me in the market at lunchtime and even, when I cycle home, the driver who cuts me up? A tall order indeed.

Quakers have long had objections to titles denoting status. I do not have a problem with honouring people who are outstanding in the community, the arts and sport. Still, it makes me angry to see the perpetuation of class in the honours system. Leaving aside the Lords, Sirs and Dames, just consider MBEs, OBEs and CBEs. BE stands for British Empire, an anachronism and a form of rule which holds some nationalities and races superior to others. To this day, whether someone becomes a Member, an Officer or a Commander of the British Empire depends more on class than contribution.

This may seem a trivial example, but it illustrates how inequality is still accepted as the way of the world. It hardly seems surprising then that more significant injustices persist. People may be repelled at the idea of slavery and rarely call children "illegitimate" these days, but many talk about "illegal" migrants and accept that foreign nationals may be kept in detention without trial. But terms like these, and "asylum seeker", are often used where racist sentiments are felt but not expressed. And the gap in wealth between the rich and the poor keeps growing.

The Quaker way offers a different vision, even when we fall short in practice. I remember noticing what happened when a man who had chaired the annual meetings of British Quakers finished his term in that role. One day he was up on the podium, the next he had found a new service, on the floor of the meeting as microphone steward.

As long as inequality exists in people's minds and discrimination continues in word and deed, the Quaker testimony to equality remains needed and precious.

8

Writing about my journey to and within Quakers will, I think, illustrate what the Quaker testimony to equality has taught me about myself and how I live in the world. I can't claim that Quakers have all the answers and that they get it right all the time, but my experience of being accepted for who I am has allowed me to explore my spirituality and my journey with others.

I was brought up in a liberal-thinking family in terms of both politics and morals: an unusual family I thought at the time, but perhaps all families are unusual. From an early age, ideas of people being equal were the norm in how we were shown the world. There was also an expectation that, in religion as in all other aspects of life, I had to find my own way and my parents would not influence my choices.

In my teens, living in a provincial town, I realised that I was very different from others around me. I had no language that could describe this difference, and so being a sixteen-year-old gay teenager in the 1970s was not an easy state to be in. I was unable to express myself, fearful of what others might think, guilty about my own feelings. Over subsequent years I grew to realise that difference was not the important issue and that this was who I was. I grew to realise that I could be proud of myself as an individual and that if people did not accept me, then this was their problem, not mine.

My view of religion was firmly based on the fact that as a gay man I would not be welcomed in most churches and that at the very best I would be tolerated. I loathe being tolerated. In a strange way it made me angry, not only towards the religion, but also towards God. I knew nothing of Quakers at the time and I was very much out in the wilderness as far as a spiritual life was concerned. Perhaps I was excluding myself.

I found myself needing to explore something within me that had come out of my professional life. I was working with people who were dying and who faced exclusion from society. I wanted to find somewhere where I would be accepted for who I was, and where I would not be judged. I found myself coming to a Quaker meeting and being welcomed. It soon became clear that these people were interested in who I was as an individual and what I could offer to the meeting. My sexual orientation appeared not to matter. This was a revelation. My anger began to dissipate.

I have learnt that while there are many differences among people – and this needs to be celebrated – when we come together in worship we are all equal. This has not always been easy for me as I still feel anxiety and even anger towards other churches who profess that being gay is evil, or that it can be treated like a disease.

I learnt a great deal about living through Testimony when I attended a meeting of eight hundred people who had come together to discuss *Quaker Faith & Practice*, our Quaker book of discipline. The subject was whether to include sections written by gay people about their relationships. There were all kinds of concerns expressed about this issue. Some people felt uncertain, others welcomed it. One speaker was extremely hostile. Eventually, that hostility convinced the meeting to include all the sections under consideration. I was deeply moved.

"Love is the hardest lesson in Christianity; but, for that reason, it should be most our care to learn it." These words by William Penn showed me that I had to learn love for those who found my sexual orientation difficult. I've done this by trying to understand where these people come from, modifying my attitude towards them and being less defensive in my approach.

I have realised that my sexuality is only a part of who I am. I am made up of many other parts that can't be sectioned off. They all have equal status in making the person that I am.

9

Long before I came to Quakers I had embraced, or at least tried to embrace, the value of equality, meaning not that everyone is the same, but that they deserve equal regard. I had practised a Buddhist meditation on "loving kindness", where we are asked to bring together in our mind someone that we like, that we dislike, that we hardly know and ourselves, on an equal basis. At work I had helped the push towards a fairer distribution of resources within the NHS. More personally, I always enjoyed the inclusiveness of the Health Service, the amazing mixture of people passing through any inner city hospital. So when I joined the Quakers, the testimony to equality seemed an easy one to embrace. But actually I have encountered some surprises and problems.

My main problem was around the word "God". Central to the Quaker testimony to equality is the view that all people can access God directly, and that we can answer that of God in everyone. But I have no sense of God as a being with whom it is possible to have a personal relationship. What I do have is a conviction that there is a spiritual dimension to life, and that this is manifest in many ways: in the awesome mystery of the cosmos; in beauty in nature and art; in our sense of values; in the extraordinary courage, dignity and love that human beings can show; in the sense of timelessness and presence that many people experience. Interpreting "God" in this way, the testimony makes complete sense to me. For instance, it asks us to be open to that of God even in those who torture, abuse, or make war on others. I wonder whether anyone can reach the point where everything is worthless and nothing matters?

One example of equality in action is that Quakers with very different beliefs respect each others' views and the experience on which they are based. I was therefore shocked when someone ministered in Meeting that he felt sorry for agnostics and atheists. He wasn't empathising with us because we were sad; he was pitying us because he had something better. This brought home to me just what an arrogant and hurtful thing pity is.

Another shock, but a nice one, was discovering how Quakers run business meetings. All my working life I went to meetings knowing what I wanted to be agreed and fighting my corner to achieve it. But in Quaker meetings for business, people who wish to speak do so in turn and each is listened to carefully. There is no voting; the clerk draws out the feeling of the meeting and if there is none the subject is revisited later. So I go into a meeting without my mind made up, and my initial ideas often change. It's slow, but it works!

Sometimes I think the idea of equality is misinterpreted. For instance, there were protests when we set up a women's group in our meeting because this excluded men, but our point was that a women's group functions differently from a mixed one – or, I am told, a men's one. Equality is surely about respecting and responding to differences, not treating everyone the same.

Despite such odd hiccups I have found that the testimony to equality really does lead to tolerance and mutual respect within my local Quaker community, and happier personal relationships. This has made me realise how relevant these values are to society generally. The prospects, however, seem bleak. Modern capitalism pushes us all the time to want and compete for more and more material goods. Yet there is good evidence that, once basic needs are met, what determines the level of happiness in a society is not its wealth, but the degree of equality enjoyed by its members. I remember in Bhutan being amazed at how much people smiled and laughed. The king of this Buddhist country has made "gross national happiness" the nation's objective, and it seems that Bhutan, whilst being one of the poorest countries in the world, is also one of the happiest. Our testimony to equality is perhaps one of the most valuable things that Quakers have to offer today.

10

As a Quaker my commitment to the inclusion and equality of all people is based on the claim that every person has the potential to encounter a direct experience of God and that experience has the power to change and transform us.

Such conviction challenges how I am to be in relation to others. I try to be aware of this potential in everyone I meet and to respond to it, to nurture it, to encourage it. I try not to label, categorise, dismiss, nor give worth to one person more than another. I try to go beyond the outward appearance and to relate to that person honestly, fully, wholeheartedly. I have to treat myself in the same way too and not feel inferior or superior to anyone else.

There is for me a difference between this religious conviction and the political claim for the equal rights of all. All people clearly do not share equally in the resources and power of the world and I am challenged to engage in actions which give rise to genuine social justice for all. I believe the expression of equal opportunities is an empty gesture unless I refrain from making prejudiced judgements about the different life journeys of others, and embrace those of different gender, sexual orientation, power status, religion, culture, and all abilities.

As a child I learnt something of the work of the Quakers William Howard and Elizabeth Fry and their concern to address the appalling conditions of the prisons at that time. I felt a piercing rage at the injustice of those who were so badly treated. I was inspired by these reformers as they improved the conditions and the self-respect of the men, women and children who were imprisoned. Later I learnt that Elizabeth Fry was a determined, feisty woman who cajoled and challenged the authorities and the women prisoners to make the changes she believed were necessary. No sweet, gentle do-gooder was she, but realistic, visionary and capable.

Why do prisons concern me now as a Quaker? "The degree of civilisation in a society can be judged by entering its prisons," wrote Dostoevsky in *The House of the Dead*. I am dismayed that the UK has one of the highest rates of imprisonment in the world. I have witnessed how the criminal justice system prevents the full potential of many offenders.

I was for many years a prison visitor at a large local prison. I witnessed that many prisoners had high levels of illiteracy and mental health problems; many had been disadvantaged and abused as children; many were addicted to drugs which determined their behaviour and offences.

Offenders are daily abused with rough judgement in the popular media, and little understanding is sought for the complex reasons for their offences. I know that, just as in the wider society, there is variety in prisoners' behaviour: some are damaged people, some are likeable rogues, others have genuine remorse for their actions, others can be manipulative and mean.

Education, family relationships – particularly with their children – and rehabilitation programmes can provide the motivation to change. I believe that being treated with respect is a powerful tool of encouragement to change, and everyone has the potential to realise their full self-respect.

Many prison officers I observed relate to those in their custody with fairness and affirmation of genuine efforts of "good" behaviour. The staff who are entrusted with the daily care of those we imprison are often reviled by the wider community. It is not a job to mention lightly in social company.

In our community justice system there is need for some prisons, for those who can best address their violent and destructive behaviour in a secured environment and to protect others from harm. But why as a society do we prefer to pay the huge costs of a system that does not work for so many offenders, whilst many alternative strategies for reparation, amendment and restoration are neither explored nor funded?

Many intelligent and resourceful people have made strenuous efforts to address these issues and do important work to promote a more effective community justice system. Many Quakers support the work of the Prison Reform Trust and similar bodies. Some Quakers work within the penal system to contribute towards a just and fair response to offenders. Others volunteer with Victim Support and with prisoners' families' support groups. Some are appointed Quaker prison ministers while others volunteer as prison visitors.

If the Quaker saying that "each person is unique, precious, a child of God" is true, then I believe it to be the most radical statement for working towards equality and inclusion. I can begin every encounter with another person with the possibility of receiving a divine revelation of insight and a learning experience. Such expectancy is the joy of my Quaker spiritual path.

11

I was brought up to value education highly. This was not education as an end in itself, but as a means of continuing my family's journey out of working-class grind to middle-class gentility. This started with my grandfathers, who carried Protestant values of hard work and self-improvement to their logical conclusion. The rich are rich because they work hard and the poor are poor because they are lazy or lack initiative. And as for the idle rich, well, er... inequality is part of God's divine plan.

I absorbed this thinking because it was all around me like the air we breathe. This is Calvinism: wealth is a sign you are one of a predestined elect, failure that you are not. A typical phrase I would hear is "God helps those who help themselves", quoted as though from the Bible (it isn't, by the way). Many in my family worship in this tradition so are close to this mindset, but I am convinced this thought system has been completely absorbed into the Western psyche and is the main basis of our passive acceptance of inequality. Indians have their caste system, and the Chinese have fortune. Few cultures exist that don't have some method of justifying inequality.

I am thankful my Anglican school education revealed a very different interpretation of the Christian faith; one which was concerned with putting others before ourselves, helping the stranger, and being humble. We were also encouraged to be competitive, with the warning that failure in the classroom would lead to a poor and boring life, so the good was undone and the message contradictory as it is in most churches. When the pressure to succeed became too great, I rebelled by questioning this whole value system. I was familiar with Christianity, so turned to the Bible as a teenager.

I was shocked and delighted to discover that Jesus and his immediate followers were strongly opposed to the worldly ambitions that had been drummed into me and caused so much anxiety. Inequality is rejected in all its forms: the wealthy person's attachment to private property is a massive hindrance to salvation; professing a particular religion earns no points, but only those whose hearts are changed can truly know God; in Christ, race and gender are irrelevant.

This kind of Christianity, the kind found in the Bible, the early Church and in your own heart, is hard to find elsewhere. But another "Christianity", which accepts violence and inequality, and elitist notions of salvation, one which accommodates our selfish instincts, is everywhere. Given the choice between a tough-going life of self-denial or one which is comfortable and secure, the majority are likely to go for the latter, especially if that is the main thing on offer. No surprises there. The problem, the real problem with being wealthy, racially supremacist, or thinking being male gives you special authority, is not so much that you are obstructing modern democracy. The real problem is that you are deluded and mistake yourself for God.

God loves all his people equally. And even if you don't have a faith, there can be no denying that great equalising experience of death. At the end of the day we all end up in the same place. Even as a child I found this thought oddly comforting and realised that my successes and failures don't really matter. This gave me a little refuge, but a deeper lasting peace eluded me until later.

Quakers showed me the stupid attitudes I held on to: the way I would look down (in subtle ways) on supposed inferiors, or admire supposed superiors, but that was just the start. I already knew this was wrong, but the power of social conditioning makes it virtually impossible to act in any way other than the one people expect us to. The real gift they gave me was to show me an opposite power, the inward conditioning of Christ within, firstly as the Light that reveals my deluded state, and then the Power to re-orientate my heart and mind away from other people's view of me and toward God.

I have hardly started this journey, but there has been progress. I know a measure of peace that I had not known before. In a small way this has enabled God to use me to make his world a better place. There is no need to be modest about that. It's God's work, not mine.

The cleaner (I don't know her name) who vacuums round my feet as I stay on late at work to write this piece is part of an invisible world of people who "do" for the rest of us. She is on the bottom end of the pay scale because her work is thought to be less important than mine. She has virtually no say in the running of the workplace. This is completely wrong, but so great is our delusion it would be considered dangerous to have it any other way. Modern liberal democracy won't change this, as it is designed to protect the wealthy and powerful. But as God's Kingdom is formed on earth – and it is, little by little – the veil is being lifted and justice is coming.

12

Everyone is equal in the human condition. Or, if you prefer, we are all equal before the Divine: unique, precious, children of God. We are all born. We all experience suffering and pain; most know joy and love, and perhaps the presence of God. We all die. Naked came I out of my mother's womb, and naked shall I return thither. In death there are no distinctions of class, race, gender or wealth. As my auntie used to say: there are no pockets in shrouds.

This acceptance of equality is an obvious truth to Quakers. Although we have no creeds, no set form of words to abide by, there are certain truths at which we do all arrive when we worship together, when, in stillness, we open ourselves to the eternal Divine. These we call testimonies, and they inform the way we try to live our lives, and how we treat other people. Equality is one of these testimonies, and perhaps the most basic of them.

There are many facets to the testimony to equality, but it was gender equality among Quakers that was one of the first to impress me personally. I had grown up in a church in which the clergy was entirely male, from the bishops down to the pastors of the smallest churches. In addition to this hierarchical, male, structure there was a congregational element, and some decisions affecting the individual church were decided by a vote of its members. Its male members, that is. As a thirteen-year-old girl I was told that I would have influence in the church rather than a vote. This influence would be exercised through my father, my husband (for such there would surely be) and my brothers. My brothers! Surely this was some sort of joke.

It was a joke from which I did not recover. When I had left that church far behind and discovered Quakers, in my early twenties, one of the things I most valued was the equal status of men and women in the organisation. I was delighted to find that I was wholly accepted as a woman, and there was no aspect of church affairs from which I would be excluded because of my sex. I was accepted in my own right; my successes and failures were due to me as a person, not as a woman.

And this had been the case from the earliest days of the Quaker movement, in the mid-seventeenth century, when women ministered, and travelled in the ministry, in the same way as men. Although there were separate men and women's business meetings, women were never treated as spiritually second rate. And although it is true that in present-day Quaker meetings catering committees tend to have more female members than do finance committees, there is no office in the Society from which a woman is debarred. Men and women play an equal part in our Meetings for Worship, with no hierarchical structure of any sort. We are equal in our business meetings, and in our witness in the world. No one's talents are lost because of gender requirements for specific positions.

Although the repression of women in religious bodies has always been a reflection of their role in society at large, there have, of course, always been theological bases put forward to justify it. Traditionally, it has been found in the misogynist statements of Paul in the New Testament epistles, especially, famously, his injunction in Corinthians to women to keep silent in the church. (Might this not be a plea to women to stop gossiping during the service, sometimes to be found in the present-day Greek church?) Less frequently quoted is the passage in Paul's letter to the Galatians: "There is neither Jew nor Greek, there is neither bond nor free, there is neither male nor female: for you are all one in Christ Jesus." Scripture can indeed be made to support arguments on either side of most given issues.

As abuses of women in the world go, just failing to be given a voice or a role in a religious body may seem slight. Many women live in cultures where their basic freedoms are severely curtailed. They may be imprisoned in their homes; deprived of education and health care; raped, beaten, and even killed with impunity.

Women are not a minority and yet have long suffered repression and discrimination in all cultures, being vulnerable as the bearers and carers of infants. For me, it is one thing to have this be the case in society at large. To have it as a judgement on my ability to experience the Divine, my relationship with God, is another, intolerable thing. And as a Quaker woman, I don't have to put up with it.

What do you feel about equality?

WHAT ABOUT EVIL?

My inward sufferings were heavy... The Lord showed me that the natures of those things which were hurtful without, were within in the hearts and minds of wicked men... I cried to the Lord, saying, "Why should I be thus, seeing I was never addicted to commit those evils?"

And the Lord answered that it was needful I should have a sense of all conditions, how else should I speak to all conditions; and in this I saw the infinite love of God.

I saw also that there was an ocean of darkness and death, but an infinite ocean of light and love, which flowed over the ocean of darkness. And in that also I saw the infinite love of God.

George Fox, one of the first Quakers, writing in 1647

1

Like you, I am capable of committing terrible wrongs. And like you – at least, I assume that we're alike in this respect – I spend my life doing what I can not to commit them. Perhaps you don't have to struggle as much as I sometimes do, but I'm prepared to bet that there have been times when you have been tempted to give in to the destroyer.

There is a destroyer inside me. It wasn't there when I came into the world. Like many Quakers, I believe that we are born not, as some religious people might have it, suffering under a cruel burden of Original Sin, but rather basking in the joy of Original Blessing. And that blessing has stayed with me, however difficult my life has been. I experienced a lot of hostility and aggression as a child. As a result I became tormented by infantile jealousy, a paralysing fear of my parents and a cold preoccupation with death. I remember becoming aware at quite an early age of what I now think of as a darkness growing slowly inside me.

The darkness was not of my making, of course – many people, places and events were involved. In fact – and this is crucial – nobody is directly responsible for the dark side of any of us. We just can't help the early influences on us and on our psyches. But we are forced to live with ourselves as best we can and we are responsible for the result. The people who fit best inside their own skins are those who are able to get in touch with the love within them and live, as it were, directly through the medium of their own goodness. Quakers often call our inherent blessing "that of God within us", and it is our responsibility not only to search for it inside ourselves, but to find it. And, like you and the vast majority of other people of all religions and none, I try to find it in my own way every day.

It won't surprise you, therefore, that I just can't be doing with the dread word "sin" or the idea that we are all inherently bad or guilty or wrong. Does that mean that evil doesn't exist? No – though I have to say I don't find its presence in a tsunami, a famine or an earthquake: in people's responses to them possibly, but never in the events themselves.

Evil happens, it seems to me, when we hold in contempt the Divine within us. We become able to eliminate the need for pity. We create a world for ourselves in which we are misfits. We are driven to destroy.

We need to fight such evil. But we kid ourselves if we think that we can do it effectively by using its own methods. As William Penn wrote: "A good end cannot sanctify evil means; nor must we ever do evil that good may come of it." So we have to find a different way.

In trying to do that, I come back inevitably to "that of God within us". The origin of the phrase comes in a letter from prison written by George Fox, one of the foremost early Quakers, in 1656. He encouraged Friends to walk courageously throughout the world "answering that of God in every one" and if we're not careful, we can just use this beautiful expression as if it were a comforting security blanket. I consider it to be quite a tough call. He didn't tell us to "believe" there is that of God in all of us, or even "trust" in it. He told us to look for it, find it and answer it.

So answering that of God in everyone means first of all finding it in, say, Fred West or Adolf Hitler, Saddam Hussein or Peter Sutcliffe. It means that all of us have to look such people squarely in the eye and expose our common humanity and work with it. Demonising people simply will not do. In the process, of course, we will discover things about ourselves which we may prefer not to acknowledge. We may find that we have rather more in common with such "evil" than we thought. And if we do succeed in uncovering and facing our own darkness, we will be healthier as a result. As we consider the lives of these destroyers, each of us may be able to accept that – quite literally – "there but for the grace of God go I".

2

What is my understanding of "evil"? It is action which goes beyond our comprehension and which is unacceptable to our sense of good order and safety.

I believe in the inherent ability of all people to respond to the promptings of love and truth in their hearts. But I am also aware that life experiences can distort and overshadow that intuitive response to the Divine. I do not accept a moral dualism: God as the force of good and love with Satan as the champion of evil. But I acknowledge that we can allow the build-up of power within ourselves and amongst ourselves which is recognisable as destructive and horrifying.

I believe that the deliberate intent to do harm, to overpower and abuse another person, is the outcome of this destructive power. I am repelled by acts of horrifying cruelty and humiliating degradation, but what frightens me is that a fellow human being has a hardness of heart which blocks awareness of the other person. It seems that there is a fascination in the exercise of power and authority over another, even when it overrides a natural awareness of wrongdoing.

I can see that our cohesion as a community is threatened and fragmented by these destructive attitudes, but trying to understand "evil acts" challenges me to come closer, to find an explanation and glimpse an understanding; I may then be able to balance my judgement, to find some comprehension, perhaps even a sympathy. I dislike the condemnation of actions which are described without distinction; anything that is bad, vile, obscene, terrifying, sadistic... all carry the tag of "evil".

As a part of British society today, I am complicit in many political and economic ways which by the definition above should be called evil. I am deeply saddened to be part of a society which allows young children to be exposed to violence and pornographic images which are beyond what they can bear in their growing to maturity.

George Fox, an early Quaker, wrote of his early spiritual seeking that he "had a sense of all conditions". I interpret this to mean that he had an intuitive sense of what causes any one of us to act in ways which harm and damage ourselves and others. Setting aside blame, judgement and the culture of condemnation, and seeking to understand the needs, the motivations, the conflict of moral dilemmas, may bring understanding which offers creative ways to limit the exercise of evil action.

Why, I wonder, are some people attracted to those with power to exercise "evil" whilst others stand heroically against them? What should our response be to evil? I believe it is not to fight it with armed force, but to fight to resist it; to be prepared to suffer and trust in the overwhelming power and freedom of love; to know that evil will pass; it has no life.

God cannot be the bringer of pain and suffering, nor is this divine force intent on wreaking destruction through natural events such as tsunamis, earthquakes and fires. The God whose promptings of love and truth in my life I have trusted demands that we are there with those who suffer and with those who are reviled.

3

I see evil as a pattern of human behaviour that gathers force and can encompass many or a few in its execution. I absolutely reject the notion of a personal force such as the devil and equally I reject notions of dark forces that can be conjured up.

When good acts are carried out I find it easy to understand and in a sense to be part of them. On the other hand when unbelievably horrible acts occur I find I do not want to know too much and I am very reluctant to associate myself with them. I am, however, a part of the whole and I ask myself whether I could do those evil things which so horrify me. My immediate rejection of such a thought is followed by the knowledge that there is darkness and light in me as in all humans. It is not for nothing that we have the expression: "There but for the grace of God stand I". In confronting myself with these issues I find in myself a deep yearning to live in the light. It follows quite simply that I must do all I can to make the whole of my life an active participation in what is good.

My experience has been that it is in the personal encounter with God that the darkness is transformed. No better words describe this for me than those of Robert Barclay writing in the seventeenth century about going to a Quaker Meeting for Worship. "For when I came into the silent assemblies of God's people, I felt a secret power among them, which touched my heart: and I found the evil in me weakening and the good raised up." In the strongly disciplined response that we are called to make to that experience we are in the company of others. The silent assemblies are of God, our neighbour and ourselves, and that support is there for us when we seek to "walk in the light", in the old Quaker phrase.

My early experience of the traditional church thinking where sin is often associated with notions of sacrifice I found unhelpful. Now when I think of sin and its possible eventual outcome of evil as an offence against God I am swept into a great depth of thought. The power that I call God I associate with all that offers me love and freedom. It is to be found in me and in all others as well as outside us. Something overwhelmingly wonderful yet so simple as to be inexplicable so that all I can say is: "For me, God is." It is in trying to live in harmony with this power that I find I am accepted just as I am. This acceptance comes only when I take full responsibility and am fully present. I am not required to make a sacrifice nor do I require another to make a sacrifice for me. It is the acknowledgement that the whole of me is accepted. What ensues is the desire to walk in the light. Of course failure comes but in the depth of my being I have some understandings that give me the courage to keep trying.

I see that I need to be constantly vigilant. I need to remember that God is always there, in the darkness as in the light. I find much of Psalm 139 expresses my thoughts and my experience. I am convinced that the possibility of evil arising is reduced by ordinary people such as I am setting out to live simple lives in harmony with God and their neighbour. Some might ask, "Why include God?", and I can only answer that that is my experience and I respect those who do not wish to include God but who nevertheless are trying, as I am, to lead responsible lives.

4

During my childhood I became aware of several degrees of human badness.

Naughtiness meant doing something adults disapproved of and I
was not very old before I realised that what qualified for that
description could vary enormously depending on time, place and
people. "Sin", I seem to recall, was something usually done
against God or against the Ten Commandments and as I was not
brought up with the idea of Original Sin or regular confession I
can't remember feeling particularly sinful. However, I can
remember wondering, at the age of seven, if there was already a
place reserved for me in hell – just in case – as I understood there
would be in one of the many mansions of heaven.

I knew that "bad" included lying, cheating, stealing, hurting
people or other creatures but "evil" was reserved for murder,
cruelty and the enemy (I was four when the Second World War
began) who were, it was assumed, bent on murdering or being
cruel to us. At that time when I prayed in Jesus' words "deliver
us from evil", it was other people or the devil from whom I
begged to be delivered: nowadays I would include the evil in
myself.

I would like to see good and evil being at opposite ends of human
activity – good being of benefit to humankind and the world and
evil being its antithesis, with me living in between the two hoping
all the time, like Kenneth Barnes, to move towards the good via
"stepping stones to God". This would obviously be a complacent
oversimplification. Often my choice has been the lesser of two
evils; some of my "good" choices have caused others pain; some
actions taken in good faith have become matters for regret and
repair. I am also increasingly aware of my sins of omission – the
good I don't do and the action I don't take – what Danilo Dolci
might have called "murder by neglect".

That phrase becomes more meaningful to me as with modern
communication and increasing volumes of information, I become

more aware of the abject conditions of some of my fellow human beings and my responsibilities to them. The good that's nearest which I try to do seems insignificant in the sea of large-scale global commitments to which I am tied but in which I have no say. I want to confront evil but it is not always easily identified, sometimes because it stems from actions apparently, or even intentionally, good.

Good intentions can inspire people to give their lives for what they believe to be just causes. Doubtless many rise to acts of extreme bravery and selflessness, but the same loyalty can sometimes drive people to behaviour they would normally abhor as the vast history of atrocity and torture or "just war" shows.

It is an irony that in order to train what has in recent years been described as a "soft" generation with no stomach for war, a glossary of reassuring euphemisms should evolve alongside a systematic, brutalising preparation. Does "hostiles neutralised" really mean the same as "people killed", or does it just relieve us of responsibility?

I see a connection between this kind of gradual de-personalisation of people and the substitution of humans by machines. People and their needs can be described by, or reduced to, sets of standardised ticks in boxes. I am not surprised by the current fashion for humiliation and elimination games, where bullying and lack of respect are encouraged and admired. The implication in both cases is that individuals don't matter – surely an insidious evil.

I know that evil is an inevitable part of life and can thrive often imperceptibly by simply eroding good. This can only be countered by doing good "to excess": the fruits of worship. I like to think of Robert Barclay, who on attending his first Quaker meeting felt "the evil weakening within me and the good raised up".

5

Evil – I don't want to use big nasty words. If I am honest with myself, though, I have to admit it is what those words point to that disturbs me, and sometimes only the big words of religion are adequate and necessary.

I have seen evil in a tone of voice, a look of the eyes: it seems to be in the choices that humans make, which is what I understand by "morality". Jesus pointed out that whoever felt hate in the heart was more or less a murderer! Evil is an attitude, and you see the effects in relationships, but nature is not evil. Granite is hard and can be used to build a house or it can break bones but the granite does not choose; there is no morality in the granite. Evil would be in human actions – stealing the funds to build houses for people without homes, for example.

Near where I worked once a bomb was detonated. I must understand, somehow, what led to such an evil action. Despair? Delusion? Choice? I remember the shocked stillness of those taking shelter, but even more, I recall the bravery, generosity, the tender kindness and practical competence – the goodness – of the thousands who helped that day.

I have seen person-to-person evil and its consequences. For example, I had to watch two people I loved break their marriage apart: the destructive effects of their two-person war can be seen even today in their grandchildren. There is much I can understand (because I too have caused pain and done evil to others), and much I can forgive, but I still see the cruelty as needing a big word like "evil". None of those involved were evil people, we all suffered too, yet what happened needs to be named. It cannot just be redefined or smoothed away.

It seems to me that some bad things are so frightening that we try to make them disappear. I want to explain them as mistakes, or as the result of upbringing, or a lack of social skill. I use psychological jargon or political clichés to keep evil at a safe distance. Or maybe I can say that as an individual I am powerless: it is the system, or society, or government, that is evil, so it's not my fault. Most effective is a joke: who can take seriously medieval pictures of people being thrown into the flames of hell?

Just writing this makes me see I cannot avoid responsibility. I cannot bring peace and justice to the whole world in the next five years, but I can choose to make changes now, in myself, where I am. Moreover, I am not alone. My family, my friends and neighbours, others in Quaker meetings and churches, people of other faiths – there are many, many who want this world to be a good place in which to be born, to live and to die. The problem is, how?

First of all I need the courage to look. When I imagine the political murder of Jesus, I no longer think of a crucifixion 2,000 years ago, but see only too vividly prisoners starving behind the barbed wire of a concentration camp, grandmothers killed or maimed by machetes and bombs, people in despair selling their bodies on street corners, girls and boys flinching from those they should be trusting... Each unique, precious child of God (as the Quaker *Advices* calls us all) is here, now, along our street, in the house next door, sitting beside us, in the mirror. I need to find out facts, understand the causes. I may not heal every evil in society, but I can choose one and work on it as best I can.

There is hope in the looking. Sometimes I imagine a person: it is striking how often the people we think of as heroes and saints and inspiring examples are recorded looking at someone in a way that changed their lives. Jesus looked with compassion; George Fox was known for the power of his gaze which made people question their own assumptions and seek change. My great aunt was a strong and outspoken person who was always straight with me. I look at these people and I see the Light of God in them.

Light that shows us the evil is the Light that shows us the good. Light to me is like a laser, cutting deeper into truth. Light is like a torch, showing us the way ahead. Light shows us our gifts and our insights. When I trust in the Light, I find I do have the strength and ability to cope. When I pause in worship, I can let go of my paralysed fear, and solutions begin to offer themselves.

There is an inward Light already in each one of us. We simply need the desire and the courage to turn to that Light.

6

At the time I was thinking of writing this piece I visited a special exhibition of self-portraits at the National Portrait Gallery. At the end of the collection was a portrait of a young woman with a scheming, sly, slightly fearful look in her averted eyes, and it was entitled "Evil is Banal". "Yes," I thought, "banal and everyday, and so common in its lesser manifestations." Wrongdoing, the first stage of evil, begins in small ways in dark corners, hidden from the light, often with elaborate justifications and tortuous reasoning. There it can grow and strengthen itself. Dragging it into the light, viewing it with clarity, speaking of it with simplicity, is the first step in overcoming it.

When evil has intimately touched my own life, my first reaction is to wish it away, mentally grasping for a rationale to overlook or excuse it, especially if the perpetrator is someone whom I know. But wishful thinking will solve nothing. The problem must be faced, named and struggled against, however painful the process may be. Unchallenged, it will flourish. "It is necessary only for the good man to do nothing for evil to triumph." That quote is attributed to Edmund Burke, in the middle of the eighteenth century. Just as the promptings to ill-doing are timeless in the hearts of all of us, so is the desire to deny evil.

We Quakers are often accused of a rosy view of the world and of people that denies the existence of evil. That is entirely to misunderstand what we mean when we speak of "that of God in every person". It does not mean that every person is good, that no person is capable of evil, but rather that every person has the seeds of goodness, and of God, within her or him. It means that every person has within the potential to reach some perception of God. Like the seeds thrown on stony ground in the biblical parable, that potential may never be realised if the person will not acknowledge and foster it. But as a Quaker I do believe that those seeds never wither away entirely, not even in a person who has engaged in the most horrific deeds. That of God within remains there, waiting to be realised, to be acknowledged, and to be acted upon. To put it in conventional religious language, even the most sinful person is capable of redemption.

Likewise, we all have within us the potential for wrongdoing. Promptings of envy, pride and greed can tempt me into uncharitable thoughts or petty wrongdoing which, unchecked, can lead me into "evil". The absolute ethic that my religious perception leads me to is simple: loving my fellow beings is right; hurting them is wrong. Any action hurting or diminishing another is an evil one, bearing within it the seeds of greater evils. Thus can contempt of one's neighbour escalate and accumulate force until it results in war.

Historically Quakers have been more concerned with righting institutional and societal evils and their consequences than looking for sin in the individual – thus our stance against war, poverty, and social injustice. All of these public evils are based in a failure to recognise the Divine within our fellow creatures; all are based on a failure to accept our common humanity, and to feel the hurt of others. And although evil may start in the individual heart, it can easily become lodged in a culture, and is much less easily removed from it. Attitudes towards race and slavery are a good example of this. They were deeply ingrained in Western society, but have gradually changed only with great effort and the passage of time.

So how is it done? How can a culture of evil be eradicated, or at least tempered? Again, it is a matter of dragging it into the light, viewing it with transparency, speaking of it with simplicity. War is an example of an evil whose horror historically has been covered in a blanket of dishonesty and glamour. War is about killing other human beings, and should be named as such. At the beginning of the Iraq war a young officer, when interviewed, said that his purpose was "to seek out the enemy and to kill him". The candour was admirable, and the first step in viewing the situation clearly. To kill "him" rather than "them" illuminated the fact that it is individual human beings who are destroyed in war. From there you can proceed to question why this person is the "enemy" and why you are his, and why you should be engaged in mortal combat. And can the evil of "killing the enemy" rectify any wrong? No. Two wrongs do not ever make a right.

So, yes, evil does exist and is ever around us and with us, in its lesser and greater forms. On the societal front we can engage with it in a number of ways: by sponsoring conflict resolution, lobbying for a fairer society and, for some of us, engaging individually in small ways to right the wrongs. On a personal level I try to be aware of that within me that is not the promptings of love and truth, but the promptings of evil, and I struggle against it. "Lead me not into temptation, but deliver me from evil."

7

I think the "question of evil" is primarily about its origin and its continued existence. It is an outcry against all the suffering we see or experience and we need to explain its existence, and in a Christian context also to deal with the question of "why God allows it".

My view is that all evil stems from human action or the lack of it, and that we are all capable of adding to the evil we create just as we are all able to reveal the Divine to others through how we live. To ascribe the worst aspects of human activity to an external power beyond ourselves is a "cop out", a projection to help avoid accepting our worst nature. The devil is a figure created to describe our darkest nature rather than the cause of it.

I think "evil" is always a quality and not an entity, even when we use the word collectively to describe all the wicked and bad things that happen – "the evil in the world" – we are still describing a quality, and one of human origin. If slavery is described as a "social evil" it only exists because we do it or don't stop it happening.

The microbes of the HIV virus are not described as "evil" any more than the tsunami was, but the aggregated suffering we see raises that question for some about the nature of God. I felt the same when I was abused as a child: why does God allow this?

Now I experience God as an energy with which I am working, a life-changing spirit that can be caught and passed on.

When a person chooses to degrade another it is an evil act – but a human one. The person setting out to violate others with knife and gun expresses part of our psyche. As fear for our families spreads so moral standards crumble, defence becomes aggression and group is set against group in a collective but human hysteria. The human animal has been shown to be vulnerable to following the leader of the pack, even when those leaders are only seeking their own ends. Individually and together no outside power can restrict what we humans can do, in one direction or the other.

"Good" and "evil" are something we are all engaged with in a constant struggle. I agree with the observation that all it needs for evil actions to gain ground is for "good" people to do nothing. For us Europeans to subsidise the export of food to Africa may protect us but leads directly to many of the people there not being able to fend for themselves and to an increase in the evils of ignorance, poverty and ill-health. The evil element of this is in knowing what it leads to, not having prevented or countered these trade rules being made.

This example illustrates for me the "root of all evil" – the gradual drift towards denying the brotherhood of our common humanity, the distancing one from another leading imperceptibly to treating other humans not as we would wish to be treated, but as different from us, as objects, as numbers, as sub-human. Thus distinguished, it is possible to plan to harm, to degrade, to deprive and to kill. It is significant that Gandhi, after meeting Mussolini, commented that it had not been possible to make human contact with him.

Our own positions are complex, with our love for our neighbour mixed in with harming him in varying degrees and different contexts, and with our actions or inactions more or less conscious. Consider a person with power, an amiable politician, who may show warmth and understanding of others but be involved in the tobacco industry and so export addiction, ill-health and death, in effect, to Third World countries.

As I am always slowly changing, I must keep my disposition to others and consequent actions under review. To generate the energy to act more positively towards others than before I try to improve my understanding of myself by giving attention to the inner Light which both shows me how I am and points the way forward. To reach towards full spiritual maturity I may need to further acknowledge my own darker nature and then consciously choose the Light.

8

In approaching the subject of evil I realised that I had only my own experience to relate to, and for me, this is particularly difficult to do without, in a sense, gaining some sort of therapeutic value from writing down what I have been holding on to for many years.

The word "evil" to me is full of meaning that is rather alien to someone who was not brought up with a religious background. Do I think that evil is something opposite to a sense of good in someone? Does the word "evil" mean some sort of outer power, or is it simply the actions of an individual or group of people acting in an "evil manner"? I find that this is the most difficult part for me. If I am to believe that there is a greater good, then there must be some sort of counter force, or is this too simplistic an approach to the issue?

Can I really believe that there is some sort of greater force controlling the negative actions of individuals, which in turn creates evil? No, for me this is not possible. To say that the action of an individual is evil allows them some sort of dispensation from responsibility for their actions.

I want to explore from a distance of years, an action that society would see as an "evil act" carried out by one person on another. I am not going to detail the action but hasten to say that it happened to me and that it is something that I have lived with for many years.

Was the action perpetrated on me by another person, which others would see as an evil act, really an evil act? Do I describe it as such? No, for me, this would be to say that someone or something external to the individual concerned was controlling their actions. This was not the case; the individual was in control of his actions and had choices, but chose the one that caused the most harm and damage to a vulnerable young person. I needed to accept that this abuse was his responsibility because to say that his act was "evil" somehow makes him less responsible for his actions. He was acting in an "evil manner", "he wasn't himself". No, people are always responsible. I do, however, think that if individuals are able to act in a way that so damages another, or ends their life in a way that degrades their victim, then I feel that there is something inhuman about their action.

Since becoming a Friend, I have found a way to heal myself which makes me look at the experience, and acknowledge that this person was able to choose and that I had no choice. One of the worst aspects of this abuse was that I went on damaging myself for many years. I was angry at myself for allowing myself to feel guilt and shame; anger for not saying something to people earlier.

Can I let go of that sense of anger? I think that I can if I maintain the fact that this person was a human being who made the wrong choice. If I make this person capable of evil then I am giving him some sort of let-out clause.

How can I forgive this person? That's my next hurdle. It's about living, getting on with life, I cannot keep re-experiencing it, but at the same time, I have to put it in perspective. I have very little anger now at that other person, just sadness. A few years ago I met this person again and he crumbled and expressed remorse – that helped me. The anger dissipated, it didn't rule; the person did not appear evil and the act became real in a strange sense. I needed to let that anger go because if I let it continue I would not have survived. I still rage against "it", but now I'm past it in some way – I'm OK.

I have many problems with "evil" – how for instance do I see such issues as the Holocaust and other forms of genocide? The perpetrators all had choices; what made them choose? Where was the essence of God? Some had strong religious beliefs, but closed these off; what drove them past their belief and why didn't their belief stop them? To say that there was a presence of evil diminishes their responsibility.

But why do I not feel that they are evil? For me personally I have had to accept that the person who abused me was a human being and not something "other", i.e. an evil being. Describing him as evil would have taken away his human qualities, setting him apart from humanity and giving him some sort of opt-out clause. In some way "evil" says that he was not personally responsible for his action towards me and – this may sound strange – it dehumanises him.

9

Is Quakerism as we so often present it too optimistic, or unrealistic in ignoring evil and the great harm it causes to people? I disagree and will try to explain how I think the Quaker way approaches the dark side of life.

I do not use the word "evil" myself, but understand it as a quality, in people or in social systems, which causes suffering. I do not see it as something with an independent existence.

I know that all people, myself included, can be inhumane. I realise I often fall short of how I would like to behave. I have, at least indirectly, experienced the effects of evil personally and, on the political level, through injustice and wars.

I understand there are structures, such as governments, the global market, or militarism which, even when they have good objectives, can cause horrors. The theologian, Walter Wink, has described in *The Powers That Be* this "domination system" with its "myth of redemptive violence" which is constantly promoted as inevitable and right.

One response to evil is escapism. Alternatively, people are overwhelmed, paralysed, and despairing, not believing that anything can be done. Yet there is a third way of recognising what is wrong and trying to put it right. Quakers are encouraged in this by an early Quaker, William Penn, who wrote: "True godliness don't turn men out of the world, but enables them to live better in it and excites their endeavours to mend it."

I am not in despair, because I have faith that, while there is always the darker side, there is also always the light. I rarely achieve my best intentions, but I can live with my failings as long as I am engaged in efforts to respect others and to treat them well, to "mend the world".

Quakers often speak of "that of God" in everyone. By that I do not understand that everyone is good, but rather that everyone has the potential to be good, to seek forgiveness, to change themselves and to change the world. But none of that will happen without faith, not a particular faith like Quakerism necessarily, but faith that it is possible to overcome evil and to build good societies.

I am also convinced that the resistance to evil must not itself involve committing harm. Quoting William Penn again: "A good end cannot sanctify evil means; nor must we ever do evil, that good may come of it. Force may subdue but love gains." It is appalling to me how much harm is done by the concept of a "just" war.

George Fox wrote in one of his epistles: "For you have the light to see all evil, and the power to withstand it." I think that puts in a nutshell what I am trying to explain. The Quaker way, at its best, recognises that evil exists and is courageous enough to look on it. The first step is understanding, shining light upon it. What is it, where does it come from, why is it so powerful, how does it control people?

The next step is to rely on the transforming power of God. Upholding one another, with confidence that there can be a better way, a vision of the kingdom of heaven on earth, we can work to bring about change. We aim to confront evil, to support those who are suffering as a result of it, to put right the wrongs, to be able to forgive the perpetrators, to address the root causes of the problems, and to prevent the same mistakes endlessly repeating themselves.

Light can also represent pleasure and joy. It is essential to know these good things and to have a positive vision in order to bring about change. Fox urged Quakers "to walk cheerfully over the world, answering that of God in everyone", in other words, responding to the good, and encouraging it, trusting people so that they become trustworthy.

Of course, you do not have to be a Quaker to seek to change the world. I know many amazing activists of other faiths and none. For myself, I find attending Meeting for Worship and reading religious and Quaker writings give me strength and replenish my energy and compassion. I am glad to have found a community that provides me with support and companionship. I know there is a transforming power.

"I fear no evil, for thou art with me." Psalm 23

10

An inherited kidney disease rides through my family. Recently my younger sister died of it, just as my father did, four of his brothers and sisters, and their mother; now two of my nephews have been diagnosed with it. Earlier generations might have regarded this as a family curse or as the agency of evil. My family does not. We are philosophic about it, love life to the full and have observed that, strangely, the nicest of us seem to be its victims.

Genetic illness is clearly an integral part of the contingency of human life as are mutability and death. The schizophrenic and the sociopath are part of the given: desperate acts may be provoked but the perpetrators are ill not evil. Genetic mutations are essential for the creativity and novelty of the evolutionary process. It is faith which helps us come to terms with the grief and suffering of this inexorable process, and love which enables us to support others in the midst of it. Our hope lies in the developments and priorities of medical research.

In the same way I look with ambivalent horror at the latest global calamities. They are expressions of the nature of our planet. Movements of tectonic plates over millions of years have been responsible for many major environmental changes that have affected the human story. However appalling in terms of loss of life and homes and even civilisations, they are also part of the contingency of life on our living earth, not evil or supernatural.

The evidence is overwhelming that God has never stepped in to alter the material conditions of the world, whether plague, tsunami or Holocaust. In this sense I do not understand God as Love, rather I see God as All. More helpfully I see God as Source or Divine Energy – a deeper and more subtle power which our human consciousness, or soul, resonates with. From this inner agency of Light, the emerging attributes of human caring and compassion, typified by Jesus, show an evolving new way. God's hands are our hands: witness the immediate flood of disaster aid. Intelligent humanity could put its resources into tsunami detection and warning systems not armaments, and think twice about building on seismic fault lines and active volcanoes.

So what is evil? I am persuaded it is solely human, an excess of human badness, a person's spiritual breakdown. It evokes horror and repulsion but needs to be understood; calling it metaphysical diminishes our responsibility. Devils and demons are human projections of our infantile rages and obsessions, more relevant in theatre than theology. Rogue animals can be vicious, but lacking an overt moral framework that comes with language and community, they are not evil, however terrifying. Our human spirituality, our self-consciousness, distinguishes us from the primates and from instinct. This spirituality is intrinsic to the evolving biological organism for generating meaning and binding community. But when it splits off and the ego overwhelms the controlling and emerging Self then we become worse than rogue animals for we lack even instinctual control.

Fortunately I have no intimate experience of evil. Yet I have lived my entire life in its shadow, on the fringes of war. As a child in the 1940s I was terrified by the London bombings, felt estranged in the years of evacuation, and have been emotionally caught up in the spate of international barbarities and genocides since, often shamefully blessed by "my" government. An axis of evil is surely a metaphor oblivious to bombs?

The root of the problem is power. The experience and feeling of power inflates and exaggerates our spiritual, inner-world state – whether within a family, a like-minded group or in the leadership of a nation. When we feel like a God, or feel we are the agent of God, especially in the pursuit of a utopian religious or political dream, then we start behaving demonically. All of us have some kind of addiction, some dimension of our feeling which most gives us a buzz. From this we know the temptation to go one more step than last time, to cross a barrier, to realise that we have got away with it without harm or discovery: so we take another step. We are curious creatures and this pattern could be for the good, if we are a scientist or artist at the cutting edge of our field, but in terms of our personal addiction it can lead to culpability, exposure and ruin.

The process of doing bad deeds runs the same course: none of us is immune from such allurement. A small first step into illegality and non-detection, a second and a third and so we find ourselves in a state of excess: into evil acts. The Enron bankruptcy was classic: the greater the power the greater the risk of spiritual inflation. For politicians in power the risk is enormous. The great evils of environmental desecration and multi-national fraud have been politically encouraged and condoned.

The declaration of war is the greatest responsibility any human being ever has to make. To decide it almost alone as most dictators and tyrants will, even within a democracy, is an invitation to unleash all civilising constraints. In the excesses of legitimised torture, rape and plunder evil grows rampant, with revenge inevitable. Today evil more robustly stalks the corridors of power than it flourishes in the disturbed heart of the rare serial killer. Power creates the right conditions for evil to become contagious. Without exception we all have the potential to get caught up in it. It also is part of our genetic inheritance that requires doctors of the spirit.

The spiritual way brings fruits of forgiveness and reconciliation. They need preparation and nurture, along with the courage to understand the triggers and breeding grounds of evil. Curtailing and taking responsibility for power may be our greatest spiritual challenge.

11

At my school for the daughters of missionaries, I was the school atheist. The horrors of the Holocaust were just emerging. My passionately held view was that, if there was a good and all-powerful God, he (definitely he in those days) would not allow such evil in the world. The reply was that evil was our fault, not God's, because we had free will and chose evil. We sang hymns about how all good things came from God, and all bad ones came from us. I thought, and still think, that this position is sad and absurd. People of their own choice show incredible love and courage, and do wonderful things as well as horrible ones. Either these are both our responsibility, or both are determined by the nature of the universe. Maybe both these things are true: we do what we do from choice, but how we choose lies in the way that life, including ours, has evolved on this planet.

My position now is much more agnostic. It's hard to accept, but there seem to be a lot of questions we just can't answer. The Buddha taught that there are some questions that it is not useful to ask, such as whether the soul is the same as the body or another thing, whether the universe is infinite and eternal. Stephen Pinker, in *How the Mind Works*, has a more up-to-date list of mysteries which may, for us, be unsolvable, including consciousness, free will and morality. To this list I would add whether there are forces for good or evil which are in some way external to ourselves; and whether good and evil are equally strong or good is ultimately stronger.

So if metaphysical speculation is useless, what do I feel that I do know? First that there is evil; we have to accept that it exists.

Second, to me, the essence of evil is deliberately harming others; but I have to accept that many people have moral codes which regard other actions as evil, for instance blasphemy and homosexuality. There are also complex issues about what we do to animals, which there is not space to go into here, but which is surely sometimes evil.

Third, I believe that all of us have the potential to do, and do do, both evil things and good ones.

My fourth belief is that we never wholly know what drives others to make the choices they do; we should not regard the person as evil, but the action. This has implications for justice; its aims should surely be to prevent and deter crime, rehabilitate the criminal, and help the victim, but not punishment – inflicting harm for its own sake. The problem here is that forgiveness, by which I mean letting go of one's anger, is difficult, and retribution is often an important aid to the victim; this has to be taken into account. In one's own internal world, the knowledge that one has inflicted harm is very hard to bear; perhaps the most difficult anger to let go of is anger with oneself.

My fifth belief is that the key to avoiding evil is to regard others as having the same needs and feelings as and meriting the same consideration as oneself. A recent Channel 4 programme on the Ten Commandments and current values found that the precept "to treat others as you would want them to treat you" was the overwhelming first choice. How close that is to Jesus' command to love your neighbour as yourself! It is surely at the heart of the Quaker testimony to equality. Only when we start to think of others as being less worthy of consideration can such horrors as genocide, slavery, conquest, torture and sexual abuse make their appearance.

I have had the good fortune not to be the victim of any of these great evils directly in my own life. But I have said to others, and had said to me, things intended to hurt. And I have seen huge damage done by actions which were not deliberately hurtful, but happened because of lack of attention to and empathy for the other person. I hesitate to call this evil, but the remedy is the same: to learn how to regard all people as meriting equal consideration, and to think imaginatively about how to respond to their needs and feelings. The task is impossibly hard, but in my experience attempting it can bring the blessings of better relationships, and a sense of meaning and direction in an uncertain and puzzling world.

12

Evil? I fear the indiscriminate use of the word. "These Evil People!" screams the newspaper headline or the ranting politician about some wild, but mild, act of some out-of-control teenagers. Possibly quite a lot of what we might idly call evil can be explained in terms of human thoughtlessness, selfishness or perhaps a traumatic childhood. But am I in danger of burying my head in the sand – surely not everything can be explained away in terms of potty-training?

Are there some people whose acts are so depraved, so terrible, that they have lost all connection with goodness and are unredeemable? Is it an affront to their victims not to believe that some people, as well as their actions, must be called evil? Indeed is there an "evil force" to which/whom they have turned?

I have often avoided these questions because they threaten my conviction that all people are unique, precious, filled with natural goodness.

I have never believed in a dualistic universe where the force of good battles with and (usually?) overcomes the force of evil. From my days of scientific training I have seen the force of a vacuum in which nothing can have life. Without the oxygen from the goodness within (Quakers might say "that of God within" or the "inward Light") people's actions can be as powerfully life-threatening as a vacuum.

So – no need for a devil and hell to explain it all away!

I have come to see that evil is an unavoidable consequence of our total freedom as human beings. If there were a great puppet master controlling our actions then we would not be responsible for ourselves. To be free is to be free to do anything. The fact that we recognise and name certain actions as "evil" helps me to see that we are, indeed, "children of the day and of the light" (that's a favourite Quaker phrase again!) and it is in our basic nature to shudder at vile acts. In naming the acts as evil I still do not have to consider their perpetrators as totally evil, nor do I believe that killing them will solve problems. A good end can never justify evil means. I believe that there is always opportunity for change, for growth, for redemption – the inner oxygen of life does not go away however much anyone chooses to ignore it.

To say that does not mean that I have to be simplistic or naïve about those who do evil. They need to be stopped. But I must continue to treat them as human beings, unique and precious to God, and who still have the capacity to turn freely and willingly to Light and Life. Not to do so is to deny that same capacity both for evil and for good within myself.

And that is perhaps the most important thing I can say about evil. I recognise the potential within myself, as have Quakers through the ages. "To contemplate evil is a poor way of becoming good," wrote Quaker Edgar Castle in 1961. Better by far to attend to the seeds of good within us and help them to grow. One of the most loved pieces of advice we Quakers give ourselves is:

> Take heed, dear Friends, to the promptings of love and truth in your hearts. Trust them as the leadings of God whose Light shows us our darkness and brings us to new life.

Is evil something you can write about?

IS SIMPLICITY POSSIBLE?

Our desire to be simple,
to serve the one God,
is always only that:
a desire, an intention.
It is never finished but always in process.

Elaine Prevallet

1

I wonder whether early Quakers found simplicity as complex as I do. Is it just too easy to say that the society they lived in was not as complex as ours? Was it "simple" for them to identify the social evils of their day and in response use plain language, dress quietly, act in moderation and shun art and music?

I doubt it. They certainly wanted to show that it was not healthy to be totally preoccupied with fashion – but in 1700 Margaret Fox, one of our founding mothers, was worried that Quakers had developed their *own* preoccupation with the simplicity and grey colour of their clothes. She said that they were getting into such a muddle that "they know not what to do, for one Friend says one way, and another another". She declared their rejection of bright colours was "a silly poor Gospel".

Oh good! – because I don't often know how to weave my way through today's options either.

I used to think that an ordered life was part of simplicity. Then I learned that this was just my own personality type. (I'm the one who makes lists of things I've already done for the joy of scoring them out.) You can be sure the Good Samaritan wasn't heading down the road with his eyes focussed only on the next thing on *his* list. He's the one who always arrives everywhere late, if at all – and for this many have reason to be grateful!

Even when I think I've got a formula for action it crumbles beneath my feet. "Enough for my need but not my greed"? But what do I need in our affluent world when so many have not even a day's food? I used not to need a mobile phone – what will I "need" next? Those trees I planted to offset my carbon emissions are only a short-term solution as they will in time decompose and release it all back into the atmosphere. If I buy beet sugar from Britain I save the energy expended when cane sugar is brought from the tropics – but how else will those Caribbean farmers earn their living? Should I buy wine with real corks or artificial ones – or screwtops? Should I buy wine at all? "Moderation in all things" – but will someone *please* define moderation for me? Can't I be passionate about *anything*? Why does simplicity so often seem to mean cheap, shoddy, dowdy – downright ugly?

My brain in a spin, I discovered a Quaker, Shipley Brayshaw, expressing in 1933 something I was reaching towards:

> A socially reformed life, which rejects all that is inseparably linked with injury to others, will necessarily involve self sacrifice, but this is not an end in itself, and is only demanded when some useful purpose is served. The limitation of personal expenditure on clothes to an irreducible minimum does not release clothing for another. It may, as things are, impoverish the tailor or the dressmaker. The effort should be to promote the participation of all in the abundance of the age rather than the extension to all of the privations of the past.

Before I fall into the trap of wondering whether the dressmaker might be a child labourer, or recalling that rampant free trade will not enable all to share in the abundance, I dwell instead on his underlying message that there is indeed a Feast of Life in which all should be able to take part.

What Friends were neglecting in their "silly poor Gospel", Margaret Fox said, was the inward work of God in the heart, forgetting the Light which leads and guides. Simplicity starts with the simplicity of our worship. Stilling ourselves in the Light, we come to know "a place to stand in and what to wait in". There we can learn where our values are distorted, where to make changes in our lifestyles.

Of course the choices are complex, and we won't always make the best ones. But we can make the best we can. What is simple is that our actions should be an inner condition made visible.

2

Like all the other Quaker testimonies, that to simplicity should permeate my being and affect all aspects of my life. But it is the one that causes me unease, and with which I feel myself least in compliance. Quakers traditionally look at the lifestyle aspects of this testimony, and it is those that make me feel inadequate. True Quaker simplicity, however, is deeper and more far-reaching than its material expressions, which are not goals in themselves but rather outward manifestations of one's relationship with God. Quaker simplicity is more than riding a bicycle and eating porridge. I tend to dwell on the spiritual aspects, perhaps because they are easier for me, but certainly because they are basic to my faith.

There is an inner simplicity, a seeking after and love of God that results in the wholeness of the person, and it is that which is reflected in an outward life of simplicity. I feel that my religious journey has led me, slowly and unevenly it is true, towards an understanding of God that is increasingly simple. "Cumber", that wonderful word so often used by early Quakers to describe unnecessary burdens in our lives, can be in ideas as well as things, in the spiritual as well as material dimension. For me, it has been enormously liberating spiritually to be able to put aside the bulky, cumbersome mythology that has accrued over the centuries around the life of Jesus and the Christian understanding of God. In putting aside the magical birth and death of Jesus; the trinity; the impenetrable wordiness of the creeds; the outward sacraments, which are so dependent upon material accoutrements (chalices, wine, fonts), I feel liberated, like Jesus, to seek God in simplicity and in truth. In Quaker worship, in simple humble waiting, I have found that God is simply a force of love, the energy behind the "promptings of love and truth in my heart".

What can be simpler than "God is love"? What can be simpler than a theology which holds that the possibility of knowing God is present in all human kind, and can be accessed by the individual without the intercession of ritual, priests and outward sacraments? This is a religious perception based on the beauty of simple truth. What can be more simple than regarding every person you meet in the same manner, as a unique and precious child of God?

What can be simpler than the Quaker way of making ourselves open to God in silent waiting? The Quaker way of worship, gathering in stillness with others in a mutual seeking after the spirit of love and truth, that which I call God, is as simple as any human activity can be. Freed from unnecessary ritual, words and images, it offers a path toward God that is clear, straight and unencumbered.

So, on to the material aspects of simplicity, which are the ones that for me throw up the most challenging queries. How do I live simply in such a busy, complex and rapidly changing society? How do I justify a Western way of life that in even its most modest form is extravagant by the norms of most of the world? How much is my pursuit of simple living compromised by living with others who do not share my vision? And to what extent do I blame my failure to live simply on these others? To what extent can simple living become a cause for self-congratulation, or even a vanity? I don't pretend to have found satisfactory answers to these questions.

But a lack of answers does not stop my questioning. And perhaps my lifestyle *is* more simple than I think; perhaps my faith *does* affect my daily experience as it does with the other testimonies. I can still sometimes be surprised at how different my values are from some of my non-Quaker friends and relations. My values are simple. I try to replace household items only when necessary, and not according to the dictates of fashion. I attempt to use energy carefully, to recycle, and to use my purchasing power as responsibly as possible. I am repelled by almost all advertising, and like to think that any effect it has on me is contrary to its purpose. I deplore the modern cults of personality and the way in which they have obscured politics and even charitable action. And, as with the other testimonies, I am daily aware of these values, not as goals towards which to strive, but rather as a reflection of my spiritual state.

3

My favourite definition of simplicity is "removing the clutter" between ourselves and God. Modern life is complicated and busy; we fill up the spaces which would allow the Spirit to enter our hearts. Simplicity is a matter of focus on the essence.

So, what is that clutter?

In worship Quakers have stripped away the externals: ritual, intermediaries and pre-scribed words. Nothing to hide behind. The simplicity of waiting on the presence of God. And as it is in the world that God is expressed, a fundamental part of simplicity is to express our connectedness in a compassionate approach to the rest of creation: a light footprint on the earth and care for those who have least. As Gandhi said: "Live simply that others may simply live."

At a recent session of Quaker Quest, one of the speakers read out a list of what she needed to survive:

clean water
enough food
medicines for when I am sick
a roof over my head
some basic clothing
some paper and a pencil - and I do like my TV.

She said what a lot that was; everyone else in the room was thinking: my goodness, that wouldn't be enough for me.

For myself, removing the clutter has taken the form of ridding myself of many of my possessions. After a year's travelling I found, somewhat to my surprise, that I did not want my flat, did not want the handsome but rather formal furniture I had lived with. The trappings of my former life no longer represented the me I had become. It seemed important to divest myself not so much of material objects, but of the distraction that they represented: each a reminder of someone or something, drawing me into other worlds. When I recently had an invasion of "stuff" held in storage to see if I would want it again, I found myself disabled by it, my mind as well as my physical space cluttered.

Spareness is a vehicle for mindfulness; it concentrates the mind on the present moment and on what there is. In a prison, a patch of blue sky is precious; a single little tree in the middle of the city can be more treasured than a whole orchard in rural surroundings. Quality supersedes quantity. In seeking for more and more, we fail to understand this simple truth, this truth about simplicity.

Objects have to be dusted, mended, insured and guarded; freedom from them is a delight. I don't need things to remind me of people that I love. I recognise that I am free to make such a choice; at other stages of life it can be more complicated.

Another form of clutter is busyness, which can blot out the workings of the Spirit. We need to clear a space in our minds and hearts, as well as in our living rooms. There has to be time to be still, to allow our consciousness to expand beyond the concerns of the everyday, the pressing of clock-related activities, time for timelessness to take over, for intuition to let its voice be heard.

But letting go of clutter is more complicated than any of these. There is a story about William Penn, an early Quaker. He asked George Fox, one of the founders of Quakerism, whether it was all right to wear a sword. Fox's response was "Wear it as long as you can." It's a good rule to live by: travel in aeroplanes for as long as we can, drink alcohol for as long as we can; give up when and if the discomfort grows too much. It is in listening to that interior imperative that we grow, and in the growth we see more clearly what more is to be done.

Non-attachment, a concept central to many Eastern religions, can be more important than having less. It is a concept that goes way beyond material possessions and is, for me, where the trouble begins. Letting go of ambition, attachment to the fruits of labour, success or failure; most of all, letting go of the need to be well thought of: belongings of the ego – these are harder lessons to learn.

A simple life is not a deprivation. Whether in worship or daily life, external simplicity is an outer expression of an inner freedom. Simplicity in outer things allows us to order our inner life, and, as we become more attuned to our inner life, a simplification of externals, less "clutter", may become not a duty nor an expression of social or political views, but a mystic necessity.

In a life devoted to God's purpose, a simple life enables us to be more purely an instrument of purpose. Reducing the clutter in our lives, whether in material objects, use of time, or in our religious practices, leads to a greater clarity of vision and focus; a view of life and its priorities that is in itself simple: "The essence of simplicity is one-pointedness, an attitude and a life that is all of one piece, integrated and made one."

4

Here are some of the things that block me from God: getting ahead, getting more, getting on, getting my way, getting one up, getting special treatment, getting away with it.

I do think there are good people who are able to live sensibly with some of those. They are able to fight their corner, get ahead and still live in a productive way which doesn't harm others. Not me. I just can't do it. So I need to pursue other goals and do what I can to live differently.

When I first came to Quakers, I knew I wanted to make changes, but I had no idea where to start. Then I read a quotation from a letter written in 1652 by George Fox, one of the founders of the Quaker faith, which helped me more than I can say.

This is part of what he wrote:

> Friends, whatever ye are addicted to, the tempter will come in that thing; and when he can trouble you, then he gets

advantage over you, and then you are gone... Stand still in that which shows and discovers; and then doth strength immediately come. And stand still in the Light and submit to it, and then the other will be hushed and gone; and then content comes.

Before I go any further, it's probably sensible just to point out that in the middle of the seventeenth century when Fox was writing, "addiction" meant a strong desire, the feeling of being drawn to something. "Discover" simply meant "uncover". And when I use the word "God" at the beginning of the twenty-first century, I'm aware that you may perhaps prefer to substitute another word that suits you better.

It was the first piece of Quaker writing that I had ever encountered, and as I read it I began a long period of change. I'd always suffered from the delusion that what mattered was getting ahead. I thought that it was only by continually trying to move forward and push myself on that I could do any good. Now, here was a different perspective. Stop all the advancement and *stand still*. Stand still in what has meaning. Stand still in the Light.

When I'm able simply to stay where I am, I stop wanting what I want for me. Instead, I want what someone else who loves me might want for me. In my case, that's often entirely different from my view of things and it means that I'm forced to behave in a new way. The name I give to the "someone else who loves me" is "God".

I now live without many of the constraints which characterised my life before I came to Quakers. I think I live more simply in terms of material goods, but at its heart I don't think our testimony is about money or cars or clutter. If it were, we would be saying little that isn't already being said just as well elsewhere.

No, I think it's more basic and more life-enhancing than that. And it is a religious matter.

Quakers often say that in our Meeting for Worship we are "waiting on God". Well, that, it seems to me, is what our lives can be about outside the meeting house. The simplicity of our worship can enable us to stand still in the Light, not just for an hour on a Sunday but for the rest of the week as well. Because of that, we may be able to take decisions which are based on an understanding of how we can best be of use to others and ourselves. And the spirit of God – or Good, or Truth – will be the motivating force. As a result, Quakers all over the world are doing what they can to mend wrongs and build peace.

For me, it is just so much more fulfilling if I stare out the "tempter" that Fox refers to and try to live as best I can as a Quaker. I have tried to learn to be intelligently discerning about what I watch, what I buy, who I listen to and where I go. It's not a hair-shirt and I'm determined that nothing in my life will ever feel like a punishment. It is a gift. And without it, as George so pithily observed, I am gone.

5

The night I turned away from the church I had grown up with and refused its midnight sacrament is a strong memory marker in my search for the Truth. Such moments seen in retrospect may appear dramatic but a great deal else has usually gone on before we are able to make such a statement, and I now know that this was only one of many markers on my stumbling spiritual path. It was simplicity that I needed. For many years after that I arrogantly dismissed religion, but I found myself challenged and out of that challenge came revelation. I now knew the experience of the

Light. Although at times I have had no name and at others many names for this, I now name it God. I knew that from that moment on that I was engaged. There was no turning away. At first I could only say to those friends who had recognised my search, "I'm all right now." It was so simple: I had not understood and now I did.

It seemed perfectly straightforward. I tried worshipping with others in their churches, and although I learnt a lot, I knew in my heart that I was not in the right place. Then came an invitation to go to a Quaker Meeting for Worship. The experience itself was so, so, simple but the outcome was profound. This was not a beginning but a continuation of that elusive search for the Truth. I had not known what I was searching for, but here it was. No coverings and embellishments, just the utter simplicity of that quiet and stillness in which all are equal and no one stands between you and God. I knew it then and many years later my knowledge is as fresh as it ever was. It is right for me to worship in this way. It is here with others in a gathered meeting I respond to the presence of God. It is the living word that is found here by the worshipping group. This does not lead us to formulate statements of belief, rather it leads us to be open to revelation now and always. Accordingly it is a personal way of life that emerges, yet one mediated by the group; always open to new insights, yet having the truths of the past to guide. It is very disciplined.

Some testimonies are no longer applicable and have been laid down. At one time Quakers refused to pay tithes and suffered greatly for it; as tithes were no longer imposed the testimony fell into disuse. On the other hand, it is hard to think for example that the Quaker testimony to speaking the truth will ever be laid down. Of course testimonies are only there as guidance for each to consider and possibly make their own. Today our testimony to simplicity constantly tests me as I search to find what it really means for me. In its essence I am sure that it is about the Truth itself being simple. If I look at the material world in which I live, I know that along with many others I am deeply bothered by the abundance of material goods that are available to me. I know that I am continually required to make choices about my lifestyle and about my use of the world's resources, and for many years I have found an old Quaker *Advice* helpful: "In your style of living, in your dress and in the furniture of your houses, choose what is simple and beautiful." There is no way, however, that I have found satisfactory answers to the dilemma of being a citizen in this wealthy part of the world, and I believe I need to see this as a privilege rather than a burden. It follows quite simply that I must just keep questioning.

I have learnt that for me the simplicity of the Meeting for Worship where I am in relation to God and my neighbour is paramount. Its essential simplicity must be guarded, for it is here that the Truth is found. Generation by generation, each of us must continue to seek the same Truth and find expression for it both in our practical lifestyles and in our spiritual lives. It is universal. It is accessible to all.

In 1694 George Fox is recorded as having asked, "What thou speakest is it inwardly from God?" Nothing could be put more simply. My response can only reveal my frailty and inadequacy, though I am comforted by the beginning of our book of discipline, "As Friends we commit ourselves to a way of worship which allows God to teach and transform us." For me it is in the simplicity of that worship that with others I am more able to lower my defences; it is there that I can be open to that great mystery I call God.

6

I don't feel I have time to simplify - yet I don't like my busy way of life: there are too many regrets. If only I hadn't drifted through the years when I was physically strong, if only I hadn't frittered time on trivialities I can't even remember now, if only I had got around to asking my father important questions before he developed dementia, if only I'd said "no" more often, or maybe said "yes" instead of trying to do everything everybody expected of me...if only I had known what is really important.

Complexity isn't bad in itself, and just because something is difficult to understand doesn't make it wrong. Think of the beautiful structure of a sea-shell, the elegance of a mathematical equation. No, the opposite of simplicity is chaos.

Simplicity cuts through complications and distractions and temptations and pressures to find what is "in the Life", to use an old Quaker phrase. Or as Jesus said so aptly: "Where your treasure is, there your heart will be also." I see treasure in relationships, in the beauty of this precious, unique world, and in all those ultimate values that I call God.

My family is a blessing to me - not easy, but nonetheless I am so grateful. When I sat beside my dying mother, and then years later beside my father, nothing else was important. When my small daughter succeeded in crawling, I watched with complete joy. When teenage years brought dreadful worries, it became more necessary than ever to be present, available, in love. In the long years of our marriage, there have been times when we have had to choose and give priority to each other, and so the treasure of that relationship has grown in a way I could never have imagined when we started out. Yet I can forget my priorities, and listen to my radio soap opera instead of paying attention to my husband just come home. It seems I have to be forced by strength of circumstance to give attention – but when I do, I experience joy, calmness, delight and energy. Even the grief of bereavement had a kind of fierce purity that was painful work, but right.

In my job I am part of a team in which we are all burning out fast. We feel trapped: we try to do more and more, as managers and the stakeholders and customers and regulators demand, which is in reality impossible. The world is destroying itself through overheating and waste of resources, and in my view I contribute to this eco-destruction through our unnecessarily bureaucratic procedures and our misdirected efforts. We need to reduce the overheating in our minds, change how we think and therefore what we do, if we are to live. After all, everyone else involved surely wants space and simplicity too.

"The true explanation of the complexity is an inner one, not an outer one. The outer distractions of our interests reflect an inner lack of integration in our lives," wrote the Quaker Thomas Kelly in 1938. He had had to find what was of value in time of war and in facing other challenges in his short life. I find truth in what he wrote of that integration. In chaos I am split and fragmented; I lose my way. I am powerless, I can't decide, I don't know who I am. When I open myself to God, to the highest values, to my vision of what could be, nothing much changes outwardly. Inwardly, I am different – more purposeful, with more physical strength, more in touch with those I love, much happier too. There seems to be enough time again.

For example, doing without a Sunday newspaper and all that pressure of news and scandal and anxiety seemed such a small change in our house. We found we have more time for each other, more time for a delicious breakfast together. I read – maybe a passage of the Bible, which is guaranteed to energise me as I fight with that challenging book. I start to centre down as I walk to Meeting for Worship. The curious thing is – but I shouldn't be surprised – everyone else seems more centred too, and what they say offers more depth. The next day, when I catch up with news, my judgement is calmer. I am more likely to discern what useful action to take, if any.

Simplicity is not "doing without", but a way to find our true treasure. We are rich when we know what is important, and where our hearts are.

7

The Originating Spirit, our Source, was utter simplicity, pregnant with all possibility. Humanity's quest to make meaning of life has been a series of experiments to resonate with that Power. The finding of many is that the simpler the way the deeper the experience. There is a common thread between the silence and stillness of meditation, contemplation, inward prayer, Quaker worship and the enlightenment practices of mystic and guru. Deeper than reason and thought is the inner heart of feeling, locus of divine transformation from matter to mind, source of our creativity, wisdom and healing. The more overlaid our reaching out to that ultimate reality is with ritual, words, music and image, the more it is masked by human reality: performance appreciated for itself, not as a pointer to the Other.

These were the discoveries of early Quakers in the crucible of seventeenth-century religious turmoil and civil war. It is impossible for us fully to appreciate their breath-taking spiritual daredevilry in breaking with liturgies, priesthood and patriarchy, to stand as equals together in simple silence. That way of worship changed my life when I encountered it in my late twenties. I know it could change the dis-ease of the world, bound by clamour and conflict. For the simplicity of worship and meeting house leads us to question the wastage of fashion, domestic cumber, ambition and lifestyle in order to focus on the essence of a Spirit-led life.

Those leadings eventually prompted me to set up and work for two charities that encourage creative expression and conflict resolution among young people, and then in retirement to experiment with ways of sharing with other seekers what a spiritual path for today might be. It meant simple holidays, little air travel, modest diet, tithing of income and an unassuming pension, but they belie a life lived with abundant fullness and amazing blessings. My pleasure and indulgence is buying books; one person's simplicity is another's gross excess.

For simplicity has two dangers. The Spirit is essentially creative; its expression is celebration and exuberance, variety and beauty, awe and wonder, joy and laughter. Life denial and asceticism have so often led to narrow-mindedness, ugliness, uniformity and spiritual pride. Simplicity then becomes its own idol. Let there be beauty in our simplicity and a life fulfilled in creativity, sensuality and wholeness. Killjoy drabness and meanness as well as consumerism and materialism are evidence of an impoverishment within.

The other danger is simple-mindedness, seeing life as if it were simple when its reality is an evolved profound complexity. Originating energy, atoms, galaxies, even stars are relatively simple compared with the intricate interdependencies of the systems of weather, economics and human health. Human problems can only have multiple solutions. Beware any occupant of the White House or Downing Street who is simple-minded enough to see a multi-hued moral issue as only black and white.

For ourselves, the demands of time and focus as a teenager or senior citizen are vastly different from how they are in middle age as we juggle with work, family, religion and leisure. It's a matter of times and seasons.

Waiting in the simplicity of stillness is to wait in reverence. This is the heart of simplicity as it is of all the Quaker testimonies. Our first reverence is to Truth, the divine Cause and its irradiation throughout the entire creation. If all beings are sacred then we are impelled to revere all human life, neither killing in war nor neglecting in need, treating everyone with equal dignity. In terms of animal life, our generation is being called to re-evaluate our determination to eat meat. Today's threat of catastrophic climate change reawakens our need for reverence for planet earth itself: foul our habitat and we destroy humanity. On our one world, all living beings are one interconnected family. The call for a simpler lifestyle is now urgent; the tipping point has happened. Those who experienced the Second World War will remember that under rationing came a fair distribution, better health and no obesity. We now have the basic needs of the world's entire population to take into account. A war on pollution is a spiritual war on the selfishness, greed and unawareness that lie behind it: our cause may be sustainability but our watch-cry is reverence – the essence of simplicity.

But that simple lifestyle will depend on huge complexities to save our species. There is nothing simple in the tasks that lie ahead: strengthening the authority of the United Nations, diminishing the power of corporations, ensuring universal access to water, limiting air traffic, inhibiting the arms race and working to increase local decision-making and responsibility. Much will depend on the moral pressures from non-governmental organisations, like the Society of Friends, to increase their gadfly provocations of the beasts of power. The imperative is for our world to be re-enchanted, to be held in reverence; and for all its faiths, secular and religious, to join together in simple unity and engage with the greatest spiritual challenge humanity has ever faced.

8

For me, simplicity means not hanging on to unimportant things in a way that pushes out important ones. This seemingly simple aim involves values and choices in every aspect of life.

One obvious application is to material things. Possessions have to be acquired and looked after, from keeping moths out of woollies to arranging financial affairs. The way in which we are over-using the earth's resources is an even stronger reason for dispensing with what we do not really need. For me this is an easier part of simplicity, as I naturally dislike having things around which I do not need or value. I enjoy not having a car or kitchen gadgets, and only membership of Quaker committees is driving me to get a computer. But I enjoy keeping books I have read and pictures that I like, many of which have special associations; these are things I value.

I find simplicity much more difficult when it comes to personal relationships, and of course these are inherently complicated. Our brains are the most complex object we have yet found in the physical universe, and there is a plausible theory that they developed in this way because they made people better at handling relationships. A key part of this is being able to imagine what it is like to be someone else, to put oneself in his or her shoes. This skill is essential if we are even to attempt to love our neighbour as ourselves. So, complexity is not bad. Even so, I find the search for simplicity can help in this complex area: trying to be straightforward and reasonably open, to avoid manipulating others to suit my own agenda, and indeed to recognise this agenda and only give it its due weight.

Simplicity is of course central to the Quaker Meeting for Worship, which dispenses with priests, creeds and rituals in the belief that each person can access the Divine, whatever that may be for them. Sitting together in silence and expectant waiting is not, however, easy. My mind, I guess like most people's, keeps on bringing up trivial thoughts; all one can do is note them and let them go. Even if I only experience a deep stillness, shared with the rest of the Meeting, for a few brief moments, that is what matters.

I should like to carry this stillness into everyday life. But stripping away all the inessential activities, even for a little while, does not necessarily mean that some sense of the Divine will flow comfortably in to fill the space. Instead it may leave us open to any sorrow, fear, longing or doubt which may live deep inside us. Perhaps that is why many of us fill our lives with doing. Or, my own tactic, we can fill our heads with thoughts of other, more manageable things. At this level, I think simplicity is about letting go of the emotional baggage that gets in the way, but that is hugely difficult.

Perhaps this is what the Buddha meant when, asked why his disciples were so radiant, he said: "They do not repent the past, nor do they brood over the future. They live in the present." Or what an older woman in our Meeting meant when she said she found that now she was living "always in the Light".

To reach this state must be a long journey, and it is certainly not one I expect to achieve. Meanwhile, I find simple stillness on my own problematic, though it does sometimes come and that is wonderful. On a regular basis, it is Meeting for Worship that provides a safe place to be still, because the stillness is shared with others. In between times the spiritual side of life is there in other ways, like having fun with my grandchildren or walking past my favourite tree on a windy day.

9

When John Reynell, the Pennsylvania businessman, philanthropist and peacemaker, ordered his furniture in 1738, he specified that the materials and design should be "of the best sort but plain". This "Quaker aesthetic" has helped me to my personal view of the nature of Quaker simplicity and its importance and value.

"The best sort" seems to me to indicate responsible investment rather than fashionable makeover; "plain" indicates a simple, possibly even beautiful, functional clarity and integrity.

Our testimony to simplicity does not require a narrowing of a way of life or a turning away from the world. It is not a hair shirt and does not advocate frugality for its own sake. It is a tool for spiritual development and focus for our life and work in the world and helps us to an understanding of the essentials.

For many years I worked to reconcile the simple unity of the "one life", which, Joshua Rowntree reminds us, combines the secular and religious lives in what I felt was the almost contradictory way of Quakerism. The beautiful simplicity of the worship; the complexity of the structure which supports it. The simple shared essential values and the multiplicity of individual concerns and leadings which result in the variety of service that Quakers undertake.

The exercise which Quakers began in the seventeenth century, to strip away all distractions which would prevent them from living in the spirit, is no less challenging to me today. In the modern world I am surrounded by temptations to an excessive lifestyle and pursuit of possessions, which not only distract, but which often support the inequalities and social injustice in the world. I succumb too easily to "busyness", an excess of activity, and I am constantly perplexed and bewildered by a surfeit of information or misinformation, the half-truth and the falsehood.

I often think of John Woolman: his radical life-changes for the sake of social justice; the paring down of his lifestyle to leave room for spiritual growth; and his warning about the effects on successive generations of wasting the world's natural resources for the sake of "outward greatness". I can only try to make informed choices: use responsibly what I have for the benefit of others as well as myself, and bear in mind that I am a custodian of resources of this world and not an owner.

In *Advices & Queries* we are told that "a simple life freely chosen is a source of strength". This does not mean reduction or impoverishment, but enrichment and refinement: a distillation which brings us closer to the precious spiritual essence of life.

I hope for the spiritual discernment which will enable my life, relationships, thoughts, words and actions to become increasingly of the best sort and plain.

10

By my mid-teens I had a strong sense of the Spirit of Jesus – by which I mean the spirit in which he led his life and in which he calls us to live. Later I found that Quakers had this same sense of "the Spirit" and I now believe that every human has within them a sense of how to become closer to "God", whatever that means to each one. I think this calling is the same for all of us if we can but pay attention to it.

Quaker simplicity is all about living in accord with that spirit we feel is "of God". This is the core of it. However we reconcile our inner sense of that spirit with our personalities, our relationships, our way of earning a living and the intellectual explanation for it, I feel that sense should be the single well-spring from which we live. It is this above all to which we are to give worth-ship and to find ways to express. Like a plant we are to sense where the light is, feel the pull of it and constantly turn towards it, aware that in some sense our lives depend on doing so.

Although we will all sense this pull differently, I feel it is singular, constant and unchanging. When we respond, we are like the pilgrims moving up the mountain from all angles, each in a different place, with a different view and a different path, but all heading in the same direction. The source of this calling, the many-named Divine, I experience as a simple energy, which can empower me to respond whenever I can open myself to it. If I do so it will guide me. The call is simple in nature and our response should be the same.

So what has this sense said to me about how to live in this time and place? I decided to work in a way that expressed my love, and at eighteen I took my first professional training as a youth and community worker. I felt free from the need to maximise my income or to follow a career path. I felt that I should only take from life what I needed to sustain myself and to give back whatever I could. I also felt that by living from my love outwards, which meant giving all I could in my work, I would always have enough to get by. To the extent that I followed this sense, forty-two years on I'd say that it has been borne out in practice.

Despite the simplicity of following the one call, a call to unity with God, man and nature, doing it isn't simple. Here are some examples. I feel it includes being frugal – but celebrating being alive and conscious is part of it too, as is doing your best for your children. Part of that celebration is having the means to develop our talents or we would be giving less than we could to others. And if we are called to give to others, how much do we retain for ourselves? If we are to love others as much as we love ourselves then we would share our disposable income equally. But doesn't what we retain for ourselves also have to provide for an old age that is not destitute or a life of suffering? And how much is that?

So what have I done? I celebrated by bonding with nature whilst camping and walking and keeping fit. I searched around the churches until I found my home amongst Quakers. Then, feeling the pull of devotion more strongly, I decided that I should join a religious order and lead that life – only to fall in love minutes later with the person who was with me at that moment. Buying somewhere to live, though much advised, seemed foreign to us, and for years we worked for a community development charity and lived in a kind of urban kibbutz in London, sharing the income with others. Later, facing homelessness, we did buy a flat where we have remained. Though I have always owned a car, my bicycle has always been my main mode of travel as I love its independence and simplicity.

Looking at this issue now, I feel it is the spirit in which you live that matters more than what you do (Gandhi could not have achieved what he did had it not been for the spirit in which he lived). If doing that means you become wealthy or powerful, then it's right to pay a proportionate attention to its subtle effects on your spirit. Things we own can have an insidious way of coming to own us. We have to be careful not to take on more wealth or power than we can cheerfully dispose of if called to do so.

And as for keeping a hold on my sense of the spirit, I sit amongst Quakers in Meeting, aiming to be unencumbered in mind and body, and simply to focus on the source of the call to Unity.

11

Two powerful elements of Quaker practice help me understand the testimony to simplicity. Firstly, our way of worship strips away church decoration, religious hierarchy, rituals, dogmas and creeds. In their place it offers a plain room, people sitting facing one another on the same level, and silence without an order of service, hymns or sacraments.

The second aspect is that Quakers have always valued modesty in material possessions and social status. We like to think in terms of stewardship over, rather than accumulation of, money and material goods. We see our role in communities, civil society, politics and business as service rather than seeking power over others.

I am comfortable with both of these aspects of Quakerism. Yet I still find simplicity the most demanding and paradoxical of the testimonies.

Both of the examples I have given are outward expressions of inward experience, which is so hard to put into words. It is in essence a simple truth, a sense of unity. In the stillness of worship, and at other times when I am mindful of it, I see my own concerns and life in a wider context. I can realise and act on the idea that I am not here for myself, but for others, as an integral part of creation. I can detach myself enough from my ego to see what really matters and what I can let go.

In the Quaker Meeting for Worship I try to shed my immediate daily preoccupations, and to become aware of my fellow worshippers and all I know who may be in need in some way. I try to pay attention and to be receptive. But the first paradox is that as soon as I try to open a space, it fills with a multiplicity of things. I may become aware of the wonders of the natural world, or of little things I can do to show concern for others. I cannot keep a blank mind for long.

In outward terms, I have over recent years taken several big steps towards a simpler life. While I have done this under the influence of Quakers, and because I am aware of the strains on our environment, I stress that I have taken these actions because they seemed right for me. Quakers neither force me to conform nor make me feel guilty.

Some years ago I gave up a career with status and high income. I switched to mainly voluntary work. I downsized from two homes to one. I have become much more aware of trying to buy only what I need rather than what I want and can afford. I sold my car and began to ride a bike. I switched to green electricity. I found joy by becoming a grant-maker, giving charitable money to others who are trying to change the world and taking pleasure from seeing what they achieve with it.

But once again the paradox of trying to free up space, time and money is that my nature abhors a vacuum. Being freelance means dealing with IT, finance and filing that all used to be handled by someone else. Grant-making involves investing the endowment from which the grants are made and grappling with how it can be done ethically as well as profitably. Worst of all, I have at least four "jobs" instead of one, so that my greatest longing today is to simplify how I use my time.

I come back in the end to the concept of stewardship, defined in the dictionary as the management of the affairs of an estate on behalf of its owner by a servant of God. In the last of the *Advices & Queries* we find the same idea in other words: "We do not own the world, and its riches are not ours to dispose of at will." Some Quakers even suggest we should have a new testimony, to the stewardship of the earth.

The struggle to be with possessions and not to be consumed by them, and to be generous to others with time and love is what makes simplicity such a challenge to me, and yet so central to my faith.

12

Simplicity for me is not an action but an attitude, an intention on my part. It is not to do with what I have or have not; not with what I own or that which I want to acquire; nor is it the challenge to downsize and to embrace poverty.

Simplicity, for me as a Quaker, is the intent to give focus and attention to the right response to God; to be discerning and faithful to the divine promptings in my heart and then to live my life in response to this guidance.

I am given material things to use, to share and to enjoy. But I am also required to be care-less of them, willing to lose them, ready to let go of possessions and to trust that my essential needs will be met.

I am given a comfortable, safe place to live. Being able to offer a warm hospitality is an outcome of this gift. I believe that when we are given such gifts our response should be one not of guilt but of thankfulness, of appreciation and delight. I have been required in the past, and may be so again, to have those gifts taken away. I may then be challenged to find an inner strength to cope with discomfort, un-ease and to live without undue fear about my security and that of my family's future. I hope that I will then be enabled to cope and will trust in the love and compassion of God through others. Of course I do not want to experience debilitating poverty, nor do I want to be a refugee or homeless. But nor do I want to be uninterested in the concerns of others or to experience the hardheartedness that can come with the pursuit of wealth and status at the expense of its effects on others.

Simplicity means being informed and aware of the consequences of what my life choices and those of my community have on others in other communities. It means trying to find a more just and fair distribution of resources, even to the point of giving up a level of wealth which I value. These are the practical effects which I observe in others' lives as coming from an inner sense of simplicity, and they inspire me to follow.

The greater challenge for me is not to do with possessions but with the right use of the gift of time. The requirement of simplicity is to hold in balance the demands of life while allowing time to be open to God's promptings; to be available to others, to be enriched by creative activities, to contribute to the fun and laughter in the world. So often however I allow duty, commitments and obsessive busyness to crowd out that which I know is the way of life that nurtures a healthy spirituality.

So, simplicity for me is a religious discipline, not as a yoke but as a constant reminder to keep my life in balance. I believe it is at the heart of what Jesus meant when he proclaimed the two greatest commandments: "To love God with all your heart, mind, soul and strength and your neighbour as yourself".

And to follow that is not as simple as it sounds!

Is simplicity possible in your life?

MEETING FOR WORSHIP

In worship we have our neighbours to right and left, before and behind, yet the Eternal Presence is over all and beneath all. Worship does not consist in achieving a mental state of concentrated isolation from one's fellows. But in the depth of common worship it is as if we found our separate lives were all one life, within whom we live and move and have our being. Communication seems to have taken place sometimes without words having been spoken. In the silence we received an unexpected commission to bear in loving intentness and spiritual need of another person sitting near by. And that person goes away, uplifted and refreshed. Sometimes in that beautiful experience of living worship which the Friends have called "the gathered meeting", it is as if we joined hands and hearts and lifted them together toward the unspeakable glory.

Thomas Kelly, *The Eternal Promise*

1

The Quaker Meeting for Worship for me is a time for being still, for being attuned to the universal divine energy which I am willing to call God.

"Worship is our response to an awareness of God." In this response I seek to find a physical stillness, a mental letting go and a spiritual discipline of waiting and discernment.

Silence is a tool which helps; not the silence of a negative space or an inert state, but rather a vital experience of being fully present, focussed, attentive to the divine promptings. I stand in the Light, willing to be open and vulnerable, ready to be challenged and directed. Why? Because my yearning to be more fully my true self, to realise the potential of what I am and what I can be in relation to the Divine and to all others requires it. I have found the analogy of coming to an ever-present stream a helpful reminder of how this Source is always present and active; it requires only my attention to it to be surrounded and moved by it.

The joy of Quaker worship for me is that I am engaged with the others present in this spiritual exercise. I am upheld by them; I am upholding them. In this communal act we become something more significant than our separate selves; our worship can find something greater than our individual efforts. The initial part of the Meeting for Worship usually requires a time to settle and to find this focus and attentiveness. I do not fight the restless thoughts but give way to the intent of being ready to enter into worship.

Thoughts and sometimes spoken words of ministry may arise which inform and deepen our sense of being gathered together in the presence of God. Within this corporate attentiveness I am not disturbed by words and activity which might distract and hinder my focussed attention on God. If another's spoken ministry is not helpful to me I try to stay in the stillness from which those words came; they might be useful to others. But in this framework of worship I can keep my integrity in what I can truthfully say and do.

I do not miss priestly leadings, for guidance can be found in the ministry of others, not only in their contribution to worship but also in their sharing of insight and experience as pilgrims along a shared spiritual path.

Quaker worship may become easier when practised for some time, but I am always impressed at how easily accessible it is. The simple guidelines given to newcomers can allow a deeply centred time of worship which is meaningful to all present. It is as if we instinctively know what to do and how to respond in worship – we just need an acceptable framework and the opportunity to do it.

2

What I worship is like an energy-force, more felt than reasoned. It is singular, simple, constant, ever-present (whether I am aware or not), all-embracing, timeless, infinite and impersonal. Yet it is also immediate, available, at my core. This Oneness, this unity, is my source and the source from which all came (the millions of worlds and billions of species) and will come. It powers the evolution of all creation, including ourselves, towards reaching its fullest potential. Our highest potential is reached in the giving of oneself for the love of that energy in others.

When I am not distracted I can be aware of both its presence and my individuality, and that awareness creates a direction which I feel drawn to give attention to. In worship I offer loving attention to this energy. I am attributing the highest "worth(ship)" to it, recognising its centrality to my life.

I worship in my daily life whenever I move in the direction the awareness creates. The Oneness calls me towards itself, towards whatever supports unity in life, such as expressing love and compassion, developing understanding and forgiveness, and practising social inclusion, care of the natural environment and much else. I celebrate when I see that energy working through others, whether it's a baby's full-pelt drive for growth or an old person accepting the inevitable with grace and thankfulness, or people coming together to offer peaceful resistance to tyrants and ways of reconciliation for oppressors.

My most conscious times of giving loving attention are in the Quaker Meeting for Worship. At these times it is not helpful to be distracted by my body so I sit in such a way that I won't have to move. This means having as few pressure-points as is possible. I think the physical stillness over a period helps to slow my mind down.

As before any activity I find it helpful to set my intention for the period ahead, even to envisage the optimum outcome, and holding that intention is a spiritual exercise in itself, however often I have to remind myself. What I am seeking for are the connections with the energy that underlies the unity in life, and I do this by searching myself in the present moment.

At that moment of course I am a bundle of experience, emotion and thought and it often takes time for my intention to have any effect and to help direct what comes to mind. I have been doing things, relating to people, reading and observing, and any of this can provide me with rich material for celebration, repentance, thanksgiving and renewed resolve.

I find that the stillness allows me to see myself in a way that is not as easy without it. It's as though the surface stillness allows more Light into the pool of my mind. As I enter, it feels as though the normal rules have been suspended, that I'm both at risk for not knowing what will be revealed and yet supported. I can be slightly detached, as if I were "standing back" and looking at how I am, how my spirit is in relation to the direction the presence creates. How "separate" am I, how much in unity with the Source, the Wisdom and the Inspiration in others' lives? If I have been engaged in the search I always come away refreshed, re-energised. I can sometimes find myself blissfully aware of the Oneness.

Sometimes I may sense a "quickening of the Spirit" as my attention alights on some aspect previously unseen. I search some more for insight and learning, often with a physical sense of excitement. If I feel in touch with the energy and my experience is worth sharing I will stand and tell others in what is called "spoken ministry". Then it is important for me not to hide the light of the Spirit under a mountain of rationality, for the others seek to know the Spirit and not my words.

It is this experience of the continuing revelation of Truth in Meeting for Worship that I value most, and find most empowering about being amongst Quakers.

3

At the heart of my experience of God, of the Divine, of Truth, of the Light – of whatever word or words I can share to convey my meaning – I find the quiet stillness of Meeting for Worship under-pinning my life. For very many years now I have worshipped with others, yet it has never become a familiar routine practice. There is no sameness about meeting: each occasion is unique, just as are the quiet times alone.

For many years I found the word "worship" a difficult one, for it brought reminders of the commandment about not making images and not bowing down to them or worshipping them. Then I found the insights of Friends that suggested that worship was a response drawn from us to a consciousness or awareness of God. Now that made sense. Especially when I realised that in corporate worship we draw near with others to the Eternal Presence. This simple experience of uniting with others in the gentle stillness is the soaring of the spirit in the music and the dance.

In Meetings for Worship for Business I have always appreciated those quiet pauses at the beginning and end. On occasion, when a business meeting has become difficult, perhaps the sense of worship has been lost, and the clerk has asked for a silent pause to allow the meeting to find a way forward, I have found myself gathered up as worship takes over from the urgency and clamour of decision-making. Over and over again I have been reminded that a truly worshipful business meeting does find guidance.

In our *Advices & Queries* we are advised to come to meeting with heart and mind prepared. It is a wonderful piece of advice, though I'm not sure I know how to go about it. What I do know is that over time I have built up a routine of outward preparation. This means I like to leave my home clean and tidy before walking to meeting, and arriving there in good time with my mind focussed. I love to be in the meeting room early and to sit quietly, allowing my body to relax and my whole self to take on that sense of quiet waiting. Often at the beginning I find myself quietly excited, for no meeting is ever the same as another, and all have such possibilities.

It is then that reality strikes and I know I need to quieten my clamouring self. The poet Adrienne Rich wrote, "If the mind were simple, if the mind were bare of all but the most classic necessities...". My mind is not so easily cleared and I have learned to accept that there will often be a kind of superficial chatter. To achieve that still state of mind can seem an impossibility. However, quietly sitting there, with my body stilled and my mind chattering on, I have found the words "Be still, and know that I am God" very helpful. Of late I have found just the one word "be" quite enough. So it is that as I wait I find I am taken far above the chatter, or deep beneath. It is afterwards that I know that I have been gathered up, that the "classic necessities" were there and are there in me as they are in all of us.

In some meetings I experience what Friends have come to call a gathered meeting, where there is afterwards a deep sense that we have all been held together in the most mysterious and wonderful manner. It is not always so but for me most meetings will carry me to those places that touch upon the Truth. It is in the Meeting for Worship in the company of others that I find I have more courage to search the depths and the heights. When I am truly following these leadings I know that I am responding to God's teachings. Through the discipline of worshipping in Friends' manner I am sustained, and my soul soars free.

There are of course all those times when alone I find myself responding to a sense of God's presence. In our *Advices & Queries* we are enjoined to let our worship and our daily life enrich each other. It seems to me that when I am able to do this I truly find the life within. My efforts to maintain a constant sense of God's presence remain faltering, yet in the most wonderful of ways I am given the strength to keep trying. I often remind myself of a Friend's story of working in London in the early part of the twentieth century when she found herself travelling a great deal on the tube. "I couldn't bear it", she said, "until I realised that I could say my prayers there." Her discovery was the same that many others have told us of. In their writings Meister Eckhart, Brother Lawrence and Thomas Kelly all help us understand the simple fact of inward worship. In the most ordinary of places and in the most splendid I have found that God's presence is there in that still quiet place within.

4

One dictionary definition of worship is "the feeling or expression of reverence or adoration for a deity".

I feel I have known worship all my life, having experienced a Christian upbringing mostly in a Pentecostal framework. Even when I have chosen to be apart from any religious grouping, I have felt the need to acknowledge the presence of God in my life. However, I found rigidity, hierarchies, sexism, materialism and unthinking tradition hard to accept amongst Christian values, and this interfered with my ability to worship in church.

I was attracted to Quaker worship for a variety of reasons, at a point in my life when I was reviewing how I expressed my spirituality. At the time, I understood that Quakerism held the following values:

It was based on the teachings of Jesus, without imposed dogma;

Worship happened within a framework of silence;
All worshippers were equal in the sight of God, and so no priest was appointed to lead;
Action was a consequence of Quaker worship, which caused radical and positive changes to social structures.

I also felt ready to worship within a group, rather than in isolation.

Seven years on, these are still reasons that keep me coming back to Meeting for Worship.

Along the way, I have experienced the comforts and discomforts that accompany any spiritual path. One of the *Advices & Queries* reminds us:

> Come regularly to meeting for worship even when you are angry, depressed, tired or spiritually cold. In the silence ask for and accept the prayerful support of others joined with you in worship. Try to find a spiritual wholeness which encompasses suffering as well as thankfulness and joy. Prayer, springing from a deep place in the heart, may bring healing and unity as nothing else can. Let meeting for worship nourish your whole life.

In coming to Meeting for Worship, I remind myself of being in a community of people who make space for the Divine in their lives. I also use this space to recollect the God within me, which needs to be acknowledged and revered.

Worshipping in a group reminds me of the external God, the "God without", the divine energy that motivates us to create goodness in our lives and those of others. I seek awareness in myself of these energies, and the tensions between light and dark.

They engender life, and can also be destructive. I seek a right balance in myself between these polarities, so that I can live my life creatively. For me, this is part of the challenge in Meeting for Worship.

Sometimes I work very hard in meeting. Sometimes I let go. Both, I find, require attention. I discovered early that Meeting for Worship is not meditation for me, and for few others. It is not a meditation group, however we might value the silence.

I am present in my body in Meeting for Worship. Often I remember to use basic Alexander Technique directions such as "let your neck be free", "become aware of the space around you", and other "reminders". These help me sit more comfortably for the hour. Better breathing ensues, bringing greater clarity to mind and spirit. At other times, I may look around, and take notice of the people in the meeting. What I see often surprises me, and informs my prayer. Thoughts may swirl around in my head about all sorts of things: such as the previous week, or the week to come; about relationships. The best thing I can do with these thoughts is to slow them down, give attention, and use them as a focus of prayer.

There are often times when a concern that I have stored away or that is in the forefront of my mind is addressed by someone in the meeting. Invariably, their words bring clarity and healing. This is what Quakers call ministry.

How do I know it is "that of God" that I see or hear, which prompts me? It is not easy to discern. But one indicator is that the message is often clear, and is met with great resistance. It may be repeated in unexpected places. Another test is to consider whether any action will harm self or others, or whether it has the potential to create positive change. A positive result of action often attests to divine inspiration. Sometimes, following intuition, for want of a better word, helps to make right choices out of all the things that clamour for attention.

I suppose that is what worship is for me. Coming back to the quiet space, whether with others or alone, to become attuned to that of God.

Antonio Machado, one of my favourite Spanish poets, says: "Whoever talks alone awaits talking with God one day."

Meeting for Worship in silence is not quite as mad as it may seem to some.

5

"Together, in worship, there is a power that is greater than any one of us. Every single person can be 'in touch' with God, each worshipper is equally responsible for the quality and depth of worship (or the shallowness), every individual has a sacred potential – 'that of God within' as Quakers call it. So any one of us can be asked to sense when the Meeting for Worship is complete, and shake hands when our holy work is done, right? It doesn't matter who we are, whether we are members or not, whatever our education, language, sex, age – we can all listen to the Spirit, OK?"

That was the way I introduced the children's Meeting for Worship, before I turned to Becky and Lara and asked them to "elder" our meeting. Immediately I closed my eyes and settled into the silence.

Under my calmness, I wasn't really sure. Would two nine-year-olds be capable? Should I give them a signal, a quiet nod, at the right time? I am glad I actually trusted them, because it was a true Meeting for Worship, everyone totally committed, taking us beyond ourselves.

At the end they exclaimed to each other, "When I turned to you, your hand was ready! How did you know? It works!"

The pattern was set, and every week two of the children took a turn as elder. The elders took their job seriously, calling us back to God when needed: one day they had to speak very firmly to two older kids who were crawling round tickling our feet.

Then came the turn of three-year-old Anna. I knew that Meeting for Worship would be short – and it was, about 40 seconds! I had no time to wriggle and settle, to calm my thoughts, I can only describe the adventure of faith as leaping off a high diving board into God's arms (I am afraid of heights).

This is when I learned that a meeting does not have to last a specific time to be led by the Spirit. I was even more embarrassed to realise that I had not quite believed in "that of God in every one"; I had not really trusted that Quaker insight.

Anna's grin of joy as she shook hands with the other elder convinced me.

6

Meeting for Worship is at the heart of Quaker faith, and from it stems the way we wish to live our lives.

If we define simplicity as removing the clutter between ourselves and God, then Quaker worship is the ultimate simplicity: there is nothing between ourselves and God. Only an interior stillness. "Be still, and know that I am God."

It is the ultimate equality: everyone is equal before God; there is no leader; we are all priests: "the priesthood of all believers".

It is the ultimate truth: no words are put into our mouths by others; there is nothing that does not stem from the heart alone. Nothing and no one to hide behind. When we fail to bring our attention to God, we know it and it is pointless to dissemble, because it can only be ourselves that we are trying to fool. So, we are faced with the truth of the experience in all its fullness and emptiness.

Utterly simple, and extremely difficult.

Even if I feel that nothing is happening in the silence, I have to trust that nothing, that emptiness, and be aware that it has its own quality and potential; that it might give rise to an awareness later, or in someone else.

For Meeting for Worship is not private meditation but a communal experience. It is a collective attention, a waiting upon God, with all of us as potential channels for the Spirit. When someone stands to speak, why should I be surprised if they echo something in my own heart? Or if I speak, and others tell me that it was what they needed to hear? We are connected. As in worship so in the rest of our lives: God's love comes to us not only directly but through others; and it is in our dealings with others that we feed back that love.

Worship is more than an hour a week spent together. For me, the effect of Quaker worship is cumulative: stillness is expanding into the rest of my life; the habit of listening, clearing a space for the

Spirit, grows. By turning our attention to God in all that we do, worship can become a way of life. The American Quaker, Thomas Kelly, writes of "simultaneity": of living our lives on two levels at once. As we meet "all the demands of external affairs...deep within, behind the scenes, at a profounder level, we may also be in prayer and adoration, song and worship and a gentle receptiveness to divine breathings." To live like that is my aspiration.

7

Worship is the wrong word. With its definition of "homage or service paid to a deity...adoration", it is alien to what I experience in Meeting for Worship, where I open my self to the living spirit, that of God, which dwells within me, as well as within everyone else. This is an exercise not in homage but in waiting and listening, allowing the good to rise up, overwhelming that which is unworthy. A good Meeting for Worship is a triumph of love over evil, of light over darkness, of illumination over confusion.

My ability to worship deeply comes and goes. When I am going through a good phase, I find that I can drop quickly into the stillness, reaching a deep place of sensitive waiting within minutes. This is more likely to occur when I am engaged in a discipline of worship, with frequent practice of inner stillness as well as regular attendance at Meeting for Worship. Worship, like most things, benefits from regular practice.

When I find myself not moving quickly into depth in this way, I often find words and phrases from poetry or from the Bible passing through my mind. "Be still, and know that I am God": "Do justly, love mercy, and walk humbly with thy God": "Teach me strong and teach me true, what to say and what to do." I am also often helped at these times by a sense of what I would call witness rather than worship, where I experience a strong sense of continuity with those Quakers throughout the centuries who have gone before me, and those Christians in the millennia before that, all striving for a knowledge of and an obedience to the will of God. I feel caught up in this stream and compelled to play my role in my time, however small it may be. This can centre me and lead me to a deep place of worship.

What of ministry in worship? Like most Quakers, I have experienced ministry from others which has put into words, often better and more clearly, thoughts or feelings which were running through my mind. I have known ministry which did not speak to me, but which was helpful to others. When ministering myself, I have experienced being on my feet and speaking without intending or wishing to do so. And I have often, in Meeting for Worship, struggled with whether that which is agitating my mind is really ministry; with whether it is for the meeting as a whole or just for me. When in doubt, I usually assume it is not ministry, although I well remember once when I did not (refused to) give ministry and felt uneasy all the following week.

Worship is at the heart of Quakerism, and it is vital to me. When I am abroad and have no access to a Quaker meeting I experience an emptiness that other church services cannot fill. I know that God is with me always, in all places, but the solitary experience cannot replace the corporate. In the Meeting for Worship I can feel the living spirit working in the group as a whole, with a special power and immediacy, and filling us all with strength to bear witness in the world, to go forth with joy and love, to "walk cheerfully".

8

Worship for me is based on my feeling about the nature of God and the recognition of a continuous relationship with God. Sometimes it is prayer, when I am hoping for guidance or reassurance. Sometimes it's a quiet waiting. Sometimes it's an action. Worship is the kind of companionship, sometimes stronger than others, that I have with God throughout the day but which changes in Meeting for Worship.

When I attend Meeting for Worship I like to feel prepared. I like to be early and avoid any Quaker business beforehand. I like to go into the meeting room well before the appointed time. It is my responsibility – like that of all Friends – to try to create the stillness which will open us to the Spirit or the Light or God, whichever term one feels appropriate. During the meeting I listen and wait. As Friends know, there is something very powerful about doing this in a group. One can worship on one's own but in the sharing of a Meeting for Worship we can be channels for one another.

Sometimes the stillness is tranquil; sometimes it's almost palpable. Occasionally I have found it almost overpowering – like a strong wind. At one time I would have put these perceptions down to my own state of mind. I now know that other Friends have felt similarly about the same meeting.

I have rarely felt prompted to verbal ministry but when I have been it has either taken me by surprise or it has been a nagging thought that will not let go. When I have spoken it has not felt necessarily connected to any previous ministry and I have rarely remembered precisely what I have said. I use a past tense here because this is not a matter of personal choice and who knows how it will be in the future.

When verbal ministry happens, some may regard the "interruption" of the silence as an opportunity to move or find a handkerchief. I think it important to uphold the Friend speaking and continue to try to hold the meeting in stillness. That is also part of ministry and worship.

9

It is hard to put anything into words on paper about the core of Meeting for Worship, since meeting is a time and place of stillness, often without words. I feel I can only write about the periphery, in particular the way into worship.

I generally walk to meeting over Hampstead Heath, surrounded by the greenness of the natural world. It's half an hour away from cars, with just joggers and dogwalkers around early on a Sunday morning. My choice of route is determined by whether the unpaved tracks through the woods are muddy or not. I climb energetically uphill.

Other Meetings for Worship, at Quaker Quest or at Woodbrooke, the Quaker study centre in Birmingham, are preceded by being together with others, sharing deep issues, feeling already connected.

Advices & Queries advises coming to meeting "with heart and mind prepared". This preparation for me is so very important to a good experience in meeting, whether it is walking or being with others. The walking also prepares my body. My mind has slowed to walking pace. My limbs are well exercised and ready for a rest. Alternatively, being together with Friends and questers has already begun the process of building awareness of a community about to worship together.

Another wonderful preparation for me is when I greet people as they arrive at Hampstead Meeting House. This is a task, but not a chore, which we rotate among ourselves. I stand at the door, saying hello, welcoming Friends, trying not to thrust a hand out to those clutching bags, papers, walking sticks and struggling up the steps, thereby forcing them to find a spare hand with which to respond. I try to spot strangers, hoping not to embarrass an infrequent attender by asking if they are here for the first time, but making sure newcomers get the information they need and some introductions. I wait for latecomers, hoping not to make them feel guilty, but welcome anyway.

By the time I slip in ten minutes late I realise how connected I am with everyone. I've already spoken to and touched most of them. I haven't missed the start. I have been giving ministry, the ministry of greeting. It's easier to centre down into the stillness and community, sensing my part in the whole.

But even so I still often find it hard to switch off from the chatter in my head. I have learnt some texts which I repeat slowly to myself. Here's one from a letter by George Fox, an early Quaker, with my internal dialogue which helps me to focus:

> Be still and cool in thine own mind and spirit and then thou wilt feel the principle of God …

I visualise the principle of God as the point on a compass which shows the true direction

> to turn thy mind to the Lord God whereby thou wilt receive his strength and power

I lay aside distractions like the old-fashioned language to concentrate on connecting to the strength and power from whence life comes

I am seeking the source, the connection, the nourishment

to allay all tempests, against blustering and storms.

Am I being buffeted by any tempests just now, or even little niggles about whether to say something about the latest peace vigil in notices after meeting? Can I open myself to the healing power? Are there others here who are in the storm? Can I hold them in the Light?

With luck, I get to the point without words, begin to forget myself, to sense rather than to think, open, receptive to spoken ministry, to the unspoken needs of those around me.

The precious time passes too quickly. Hampstead has a church bell chiming the quarters. The children enter after the third set of chimes. The elders shake hands as the last of the twelve strokes of the hour fades away. People, who have already enjoyed each other's company for an hour, burst naturally into friendly conversation.

10

I wait
I still myself
I am often encountered
I am always changed

11

I recently heard Quakers described by a priest as "practical mystics". It is a phrase often used about us – and also about at least another two religious groups to my certain knowledge – and I sometimes question whether Friends have any time for it at all. Practical? Perhaps we are. But mystics? I wonder. There is something gloriously no-nonsense about almost all the Quakers I know.

Yet at the heart of our religious life lies a practice so beautiful, so nourishing and, well yes, so mystical that perhaps I need to think again. I don't know a single Quaker who doesn't find our Meeting for Worship an essential part of life. I have found myself longing so much for the experience in the middle of a difficult working week that I have sought out lunchtime meetings, evening meetings and impromptu silent worship in the kitchens of friends.

I can pray on my own, I can meditate on my own, but Meeting for Worship has to be communal. Watching the faces of Friends as they walk into the room, acknowledging smiles of recognition, noticing the people who may not have been before: all this is part of the process for me. Finding a way to sit is important, too – I want to be straight but not too straight, comfortable but not lounging, hands open, feet firm.

As the silence of the meeting starts to enfold me, I use some conscious techniques to ensure that my mind is not suddenly overrun by the haphazard thoughts that have been lurking there for days. A sentence gently repeated in my head often helps. Lately I have used a few words of Isaac Penington: "Give over thine own willing, give over thine own running...". But it doesn't matter too much what I say – just so long as the thinking part of me is put into neutral. Thinking is not part of this process. Logic won't help me now.

Slowly, the silence deepens and all in this little community are engaged in the same process. As each of us finds a tranquil centre within, so the stillness of each person meets the stillness of the others. Little by little, we become a worshipping community. We are waiting upon God. And as the meeting gathers, I believe that a subtle energy begins to work among us. That of God in each of us is encountering the Divine.

Sometimes the whole hour or more is held in silence. I find it difficult to express quite how full a Quaker silence can be. On other occasions, one of us may be inspired to contribute to the stillness – not break it – by standing to speak. This is not an easy or comfortable thing to do, yet it is constantly surprising to me just how often the spoken ministry chimes exactly – mystically, perhaps? – with what I need to hear.

A year or two ago, I visited a meeting some miles from my home. I knew nobody there. After a silence of perhaps half an hour, a woman stood to minister. She had seen a film of a sand painter in Africa, she said. She had watched him create a perfect image on the ground using nothing but differently coloured sands. When the artist finished the painting, he drew his hand across it and in one swift movement swept the sand away. "I thought how much I wanted to be the sand painter," said the woman. "And then I thought" – she paused – "how much more I wanted to be the sand."

You had to be there: on that day, at that moment, it was exactly what we all needed to hear. It was as if everyone in the room shared one psyche and one life. Something vital held us and there was no more to be said. I believe that each member of that meeting was a slightly different person when they left.

Being the sand, being the raw material, being *used* is important to

Quakers. We are, indeed, a practical lot. But, much more important, we are a religious society – practicality is of little use to us without faith. In our Meeting for Worship we are upheld in that faith by a mystical process which cannot be explained with logic. Some people put it down to telepathy, but I don't think they are right. I believe that it is the presence of the Divine. And through our continued experience of that presence, Quakers are sometimes able to become the sand.

12

I discovered the Quaker way when I was twenty-eight, retreating from a Christian church whose services were increasingly meaningless to me and whose sermons were breathtakingly irrelevant in the face of the needs of the world and the congregation. For forty years since, rarely missing a Sunday, I have worshipped with Friends. This has changed my life.

Through the intense stillness of a Quaker Meeting for Worship, I find healing, refreshment and inner growth. Vital to this has been the worshipping community. I know that those who are centring down with me, as it were in a communal resonance, have similar values and share the same vision of the commonwealth of the Spirit on earth. Early on I found other Quakers whose compassion and understanding and dedication to peaceable change was far in advance of what I could ever aspire to. So I soon became a disciple of the Quaker way. When I become disillusioned or exasperated I turn aside and flirt with other ways, but nothing has the same simple authenticity of the silent worship which unites all comers, and the hesitant words of a Friend's ministry that does not divide.

Maybe half a dozen times over these forty years I have experienced deeply spirit-shaking meetings. They have invariably been following or preparing for an act of witness by a Quaker group that has powerfully opened us up to each other, made us raw and vulnerable, and has usually come from a time of living together. They are indelibly printed peak experiences, which I have never known in my regular Sunday worship. I am absolutely convinced that the Quaker flame will only be rekindled when we are a living community of witnessing Friends, together standing against the ills of the world or sharing our faith.

So what am I doing when I worship? It is focussed in worth – "worth-ship" – in praise and love. I am expressing the worth of life, and my attempt to make meaning within it. I find it in love, both through people and through the social purposes I pursue. That quest for meaning impels my curiosity and creativity. So I attempt to come to Meeting for Worship with heart and mind prepared, bringing with me something of the deeper reflections of the week. The greetings in the lobby establish for me that I am among friends, and on entering the meeting room I try to take a chair in a different place from last week, to see the meeting from a different point of view. I take in, as I can, who is there and who may be missing through illness or holidays: some smile. This is today's community and who that is will determine the quality of the worship, for we are all its "priests".

Soon I close my eyes and enjoy the visual silence, while rooting my feet firmly on the floor, sitting well back in the chair to be ready and attentive, with open hands on my legs, the fingers just touching. I find that all of this is good preparation to be as open as possible and not folded-in on myself, the body and the spirit being a whole. Although I have never practised any form of meditation, I have learned from those who have about the value of breathing deeply and slowly, and for the first period of worship I become aware of the breath-of-the-world passing in and out of my body and all that this symbolises. At times I have said a mantra of the Buddhist monk Thich Nhat Hanh: "In Out, Deep Slow, Calm Easy, Smile Relax, Present moment wonderful moment, Divine presence." This, or "Be still and know that I am God", will help me to ease slowly into a state which I slip in and out of over the rest of the hour when I am suspended between worlds.

My two greatest struggles are with sleep and the laying down of my discursive, argumentative, perhaps masculine self, to accept a time of non-self and non-striving. I used to feel that this was a pointless activity, with no practical outcomes; now I trust that just as bodily sleep allows our dream-world to help in the assimilation and ordering of the psychic experiences of the day, so this free-flowing state of letting go, of being held between consciousness and unconsciousness, "swinging in the divine hammock", allows a healing time for the consciousness itself. Nothing supernatural but a totally natural evolutionary need and process. There is a deep therapy in standing alongside, through the silence and stillness, the greater energy or consciousness which envelops us, and which we often call God.

When I have been hurt, or disappointed, or feel guilty, or am troubled, and these feelings will not let me go, or when negativities of the week which I have repressed in busyness or denial suddenly pop up again, then I evoke – almost like a light – the highest I know of love or forgiveness, often from the lives of family and friends, and let those disturbances be soothed and irradiated by that power, "waiting in the light". I have never left a meeting feeling the same about such personal needs as when I went in.

I rarely have felt called to minister, unless it has been a teaching ministry rather than an inspirational one. But I am constantly enriched by the ministry of others and amazed at the variety of spiritual experience that they witness to. They reaffirm for me that it is not that I come to worship to discover God, for I am aware throughout the week that I am encountering the Divine as an integral dimension to every aspect of life, but that I come to worship to be in tune with like-minded people who understand the Divinity in compatible ways to my own. Together we struggle to let that realisation affect our everyday lives so that we may "mend the world".

Try writing about what worship means to you.

FURTHER READING

Quaker Faith & Practice: The book of Christian discipline of the Yearly Meeting of the Religious Society of Friends (Quakers) in Britain. London: Britain Yearly Meeting, 3rd edition, 2005

Advices & Queries. London: Britain Yearly Meeting, reprint 2007

Introductory
Ambler, Rex: *Truth of the heart: an anthology of George Fox 1624-1991.* London: Quaker Books, 2001

Birkell, Michael L.: *Silence and witness: the Quaker tradition.* London: Darton, Longman and Todd, 2004

Cooper, Wilmer A.: *A living faith: an historical and comparative study of Quaker beliefs.* Richmond IN: Friends United Press, 1990

Dandelion, Pink: *An introduction to Quakerism.* Cambridge: Cambridge University Press, 2007

Gillman, Harvey: *A light that is shining: an introduction to the Quakers.* London: Quaker Books, 2003

Priestland, Gerald: *Coming home: an introduction to the Quakers.* London: Quaker Books, 2003

Punshon, John: *Portrait in grey: a short history of the Quakers.* London, Quaker Books, reprint 2006

What is God?
Allen, Beth: *Ground and spring: foundations of Quaker discipleship.* London: Quaker Books, 2007 (Swarthmore Lecture 2007)

Boulton, David (ed.): *Godless for God's sake: nontheism in contemporary Quakerism.* Dent: Cumbria's Dales Historical Monographs, 2006

Griswold, Robert: *Creeds and Quakers: what's belief got to do with it?* Wallingford PA: Pendle Hill, 2005

Kelly, Thomas R.: *A testament of devotion.* San Francisco: HarperSanFrancisco, reprint 1996

Lacout, Pierre: *God is silence.* London, Quaker Books, 1937

Why Pacifism?

Bailey, Sydney D.: *Peace is a process.* London, Quaker Home Service and Woodbrooke College, 1993 (Swarthmore Lecture 1993)

Brock, Peter: *The Quaker peace testimony 1660-1914.* York: Sessions Book Trust, 1990

Curle, Adam: *Another way: positive response to contemporary violence.* London: John Carpenter Publishing, 1995

Curle, Adam: *True justice: Quaker peacemakers and peacemaking.* London: Quaker Books, reprint 2007 (Swarthmore Lecture 1981)

Fisher, Simon: *Spirited living: waging conflict, building peace.* London: Quaker Books, 2004 (Swarthmore Lecture 2004)

Hoover, Sharon (ed.): *Answering terror: responses to war and peace after 9/11/01.* Philadelphia PA: Friends Publishing Corporation, 2006

Irving, Nancy *et al* (eds.): *Friends' peace witness in a time of crisis.*

Philadelphia PA: Friends World Committee for Consultation, 2005

Quaker Peace and Social Witness: *Affirming the light: ten stories of Quaker peace witness.* London: Quaker Books, 2002

Quaker Peace and Social Witness: *Faithful deeds: a rough guide to the Quaker peace testimony.* London: Quaker Books, 2002

Smith, Lyn: *Pacifists in action.* York: William Sessions, 1998

Steven, Helen: *No extraordinary power: prayer, stillness and activism.* London: Quaker Books, 2005 (Swarthmore Lecture 2005)

Whitmire, Catherine: *Practising peace: a devotional walk through the Quaker tradition.* Notre Dame IN: Sorin Books, 2007

Who is Jesus?
Birkell, Michael L.: *Engaging scripture: reading the Bible with early Friends.* Richmond IN: Friends United Press, 2005

Borg, Marcus J.: *Meeting Jesus again for the first time: the historical Jesus and the heart of contemporary faith.* San Francisco: HarperSanFrancisco, reprint 1995

Ehrman, Bart D.: *Misquoting Jesus: the story behind who changed the Bible and why.* New York: HarperSanFrancisco, 2007

Funk, Robert W.: *The five gospels: what did Jesus really say?: the search for the authentic words of Jesus.* New York: Scribner, 1996

Mitchell, Stephen: *The gospel according to Jesus.* London: Rider, 1992

Pagels, Elaine: *Beyond belief: the secret gospel of Thomas*. New York: Vintage Books, 2004

Vermes, Geza: *The authentic gospel of Jesus*. London: Penguin, 2004

How are we equal?
Dale, Jonathan, *et al*: *Faith in action: Quaker social testimony writings in Britain Yearly Meeting*. London: Quaker Home Service, 2000

Gillman, Harvey: *A minority of one: a journey with Friends*. London: Quaker Home Service, 1998

Layard, Richard: *Happiness: lessons from a new science*. London: Penguin, 2005

Wilkinson, Richard G.: *The impact of inequality: how to make sick societies healthier*. New York: The New Press, 2005

What about evil?
Barnard, Clifford: *Two weeks in May, 1945: Sandbostel Concentration Camp and the Friends Ambulance Unit*, London: Quaker Home Service, 1999

Francis, Diana: *Rethinking war and peace*. London: Pluto Press, 2004

Morton, Adam: *On evil: thinking in action*. London: Routledge, 2004

Scully, Jackie Leach and Dandelion, Pink (eds.): *Good and evil: Quaker perspectives*. Aldershot: Ashgate, 2007

Is simplicity possible?
Dale, Jonathan: *Quaker social testimony in our personal and corporate*

life. Wallingford PA: Pendle Hill, 2002

Elgin, Duane: *Voluntary simplicity*. New York: Morrow, 1998

Prevallet, Elaine: *Reflections on simplicity*. Wallington PA: Pendle Hill, 1982

Pym, Jim: *Listening to the light: how to bring Quaker simplicity and integrity into our lives*. London: Rider Books, 1999

Whitmire, Catherine: *Plain living: a Quaker path to simplicity*. Notre Dame IN: Sorin Books, 2001

Woolman, John: *The journal and major essays*; edited by Phillips. P. Moulton. Richmond IN: Friends United Press, 1989

Meeting for Worship
Allen, Richard: *Silence and speech: for anyone new to Quaker worship*. London: Quaker Books, 4th ed. 2004

Kelly, Thomas: "Reality of the spiritual world" and "The gathered meeting". London: Quaker Books, new ed. 1996

Lacey, Paul A.: *Nourishing the spiritual life*. London: Quaker Home Service, 1995

Punshon, John: *Encounter with silence: reflections from the Quaker tradition*. Richmond IN: Friends United Press, 1987

Taber, William: *Four doors to Meeting for Worship*. Wallingford PA: Pendle Hill, 1992

BOOKS

O is a symbol of the world, of oneness and unity. In different cultures it also means the "eye", symbolizing knowledge and insight. We aim to publish books that are accessible, constructive and that challenge accepted opinion, both that of academia and the "moral majority".

Our books are available in all good English language bookstores worldwide. If you don't see the book on the shelves ask the bookstore to order it for you, quoting the ISBN number and title. Alternatively you can order online (all major online retail sites carry our titles) or contact the distributor in the relevant country, listed on the copyright page.

See our website www.o-books.net for a full list of over 400 titles, growing by 100 a year.

And tune in to myspiritradio.com for our book review radio show, hosted by June-Elleni Laine, where you can listen to the authors discussing their books.

mySpiritRadio